What the 𝕭𝕚𝕭𝕝𝕖
Really Does
(and Doesn't) Say
about *Sex*

What the Bible Really Does (and Doesn't) Say about Sex

*The how, when, why, and with whom
of scriptural prohibitions and permissions*

Matthew O'Neil

PITCHSTONE PUBLISHING
Durham, North Carolina

Pitchstone Publishing
Durham, North Carolina
www.pitchstonepublishing.com

Copyright © 2015 by Matthew O'Neil

10 9 8 7 6 5 4 3 2 1

Library of Congress Cataloging-in-Publication Data

O'Neil, Matthew.
  What the Bible really does (and doesn't) say about sex : the how, when, why, and with whom of scriptural prohibitions and permissions / Matthew O'Neil.
      pages cm
  Includes bibliographical references.
   ISBN 978-1-63431-052-9 (pbk. : alk. paper)
  1. Sex—Biblical teaching. 2. Sex—Religious aspects—Christianity. I. Title.
  BS680.S5.O64 2015
  220.8'3067—dc23
                                    2015015110

for Declan

Contents

Prologue

A few months before I started work on this book, I heard an exchange between a student and another teacher at the junior high school where I taught. The discussion centered around the student's choice in attire, with the teacher questioning the appropriateness of the outfit the young woman had decided to wear that day. I am not certain what had led to this particular exchange, as I was in the middle of a task, but I distinctly remember hearing the student say, "We need to teach boys not to sexualize women, not that women need to choose clothes correctly to avoid tempting men!" Somehow, this point escaped the teacher, as the teacher responded with, "Yes, but you are still given choices in the morning, and I think you made the wrong one."

Although I had yet to start my research for this book, I couldn't help but think this conversation exemplified one of the many reasons why I wanted to investigate the Bible's role in shaping society's views on sex, gender, and sexual mores—and, indeed, what the Bible *actually* says about such matters. Growing up, I had heard similar sentiments coming from others in leadership positions, whether teachers, parents, coaches, etc. Their message was never directed at us boys to not sexualize girls; rather, they made clear to girls that they were responsible for any sexualizing we boys did. (My own parents often criticized the way that I dressed growing up, but their objections had nothing to do with sexuality and, looking back at my wardrobe choices, they were right to be concerned!) So, why is, "Don't dress in a sexually suggestive manner," an admonition directed solely at women? Why are women shamed and charged with inviting sexual advances because of the way they dress? Why are they often said to have been "asking for it," especially in cases of rape, but the same cannot be said of men? Why the difference?

I had long wondered the same thing about contraception. Why do women often face negative criticism for seeking birth control, be it for sexual purposes or other health needs, but men almost always face approval—even applause—for purchasing condoms? Why the contrast? I have female friends who share stories of their parents shaming them for obtaining birth control, even when for legitimate health reasons. My male friends have no such stories. In those cases where a parent discovered one of my male friends with a condom, there were no negative confrontations. Rather, they were told, "Well, at least you're being safe."

But such questions do not end with decisions related to reproductive health either. There are many other palpable and troubling ways in which society holds unfair and often hypocritical double standards based on sex, gender, and sexual identity. For example, the U.S. Supreme Court may have finally declared same-sex marriage legal in all fifty states, but large segments of society remain vehemently opposed to the ruling. This desire to discriminate based on sexual identity is something I have never understood, even when I was a Catholic school student. Why are people who feel the same emotions we do, who have the same wants and desires as we do, but who love someone of the same gender discriminated against? Why would anyone want to deny them the same rights as people who love the opposite gender? I saw friends shamed by their parents because, as the parents claimed, their child "made a choice" to be a certain way. And, because that "choice," as they understood it, was not normal to them, they believed something was wrong with their child. As I am sure everyone knows, shaming someone because of something they cannot change is the best way to address the situation. Please note the intended sarcasm.

When I was in high school, I happened to live in the first state that legalized civil unions—a sort of "separate-but-equal" version of marriage. While demonstrating a level of acceptance, the local diocese was none too thrilled about the legalization of civil unions. The bishop of the diocese had sent out a letter to all the churches in the area, urging them to participate in a protest at the state capital to denounce the idea of civil unions. The priests at the church I attended, I am pleased to report, refused to read his letter, leading the bishop to show up at our church's mass. I chuckled along with my siblings as the priests complimented the bishop—expressing their excitement about having him there, stating that we were truly blessed—all while continuing to refuse to read his letter. The bishop, in his fury, stormed the podium, announcing, "Well, since no one here is going to read my letter, I will." I was in tears watching the other priests stifle laughs—partly out of the hysterical laughter I myself struggled to hide, but mostly out of the compassion I felt for those priests who insisted on doing what was right, even when their superior tried to compel them to do otherwise.

Sadly, the priests at my church were the exception to the rule. Indeed, the Catholic Church has been a predominant part of the problematic relationship society has with sex. But the problem extends well beyond the Catholic Church to almost every Christian denomination that wields religious faith as a cudgel—whether to justify discrimination against the LGBTQ community, prohibit abortion, perpetuate negative stereotypes about gender roles and identification, or forbid certain sexual preferences and practices. Before I began working on this book, I thought perhaps that the problem rested principally in scripture—specifically, in the words of the Bible. After all, religious moralizers invariably wave the Bible when justifying their prohibitions and judgments. Surprisingly, as I discovered in my research, and as I'll share in this book, an excess of biblical literacy isn't always the problem—in many cases, such moralizing and demonizing stems from a *lack* of biblical literacy.

Abandon all hope, ye who enter here. This book will change how you view and read the Bible.

1

Sex

The Bible is an especially curious book when explored for sexual content. Any average person, who knows of modern-day religious teachings and the very loud religious outcry against sexuality, would think that the only biblical mention of anything sexual would relate only to prohibitions on sex. To be sure, if you were to look for obvious statements about sex in the Bible, you would most likely first come across prohibitions on sex. But, with a more attentive read, we can discover some rather lustful ideas and pornographic narratives written between the lines of the Bible. In this section we will discuss the Bible's use of sexual euphemisms, the fine line between prohibition and permissible sex acts within the Bible, and how we as a society—and even many authors of and figures in the Bible—have gotten it all wrong.

Euphemism

Euphemisms for sex are varied throughout the Bible. Thankfully, in those cases where the euphemisms are not obvious, we find parallels in other ancient Near Eastern texts that provide relevant context, allowing us to understand their intended meaning. Just as two thousand years into the future people might have little to no idea what we mean today when we call someone "hot," so too can we be easily confused by slang from the ancient past without proper reference points. As an example, consider how much language has changed just within the past fifty years. Younger generations today likely have no idea what "backseat bingo" means, though it's highly likely any of their grandparents who came of age in the 1950s know exactly what the term means.[1]

One such euphemism found throughout the Bible is "to know"—as in person XX knew person XY. We see this in passages like Genesis 4:1: "Now the man knew his wife Eve, and she conceived and bore Cain." It is hard to imagine conception, and the subsequent birth of a child, without intercourse (and this is putting aside the notion of the virgin birth in Matthew and Luke). In fact, Cain's name derives from the Hebrew *qanah*, which means "to create," and the story is used to demonstrate the creative wonder in the first conception and birth of a child.[2] This example provides a rather compelling case that "to know" meant to have sexual relations with someone.

This euphemism also appears in Numbers 31:17, when Moses commands the Israelites, who are on a conquest to settle the Transjordan, to "kill every male among the little ones, and kill every woman who has known a man by sleeping with him." This is another transparent example of what "to know" means. In black and white, it states that "to know" someone is to sleep with them. A similar usage of "to know" is found in Judges 21:12, which refers to four hundred young virgins among the Jabesh-gilead who had never "known a man by lying with him."

In the Book of Amos 3:1–2, Amos writes, "Hear you this word that the LORD has spoken against you, O people of Israel, against the whole family that I brought up out of the land of Egypt: You only have I known of all the families of the earth; therefore I will punish you for all your iniquities." Later translators of Amos may not have highlighted the sexual implications of this passage, but the wording does suggest a special relationship—an intimate connection Amos had not only with Israel, but also with Israel's God, Yahweh.[3]

Two other euphemisms for sex are "to go in to" and "to come in to." Deuteronomy 21:10–14 describes the legal obligations one has when taking a woman captive during a war. In this situation, the author writes, after a month of allowing her to mourn the loss of her family, either through her family's death or her captivity, the captor shall "go in to her and be her husband, and she shall be your wife." This sexual instruction, while reading as permission to rape, is meant to mark the consummation of a marriage. This passage is a continuation from Deuteronomy 20:15–18 and applied to the Canaanites, as they often became, like any war captives, concubines for the Israelites.[4] This law in ancient warfare did not just apply to women.

A "to come in to" variation is found in Joshua 2:1–3, when Joshua sends two spies to Jericho. "So they went, and entered the house of a prostitute whose name was Rahab, and spent the night there . . . 'Bring out the men who have come to you, who entered your house.'" While not explicit, this passage has a sexual undertone. Adding to this undertone is the fact that the spies are sent from the land of Shittim, where the Israelites had sex with the women of Moab in Numbers 25:1. The author of Joshua appears to focus on the Israelites finding success, or showing their superiority, through sexual conquests.[5]

"To lie with" and "to come in to" appear together in Genesis 30:15–16, when Rachel and Leah discuss mandrakes, a potato-like plant believed to be an aphrodisiac. When Rachel requests some from Leah, Leah becomes upset, saying, "Is it a small matter that you have taken away my husband? Would you take away my son's mandrakes also?" As a trade, Rachel suggests, "Then he may lie with you tonight for your son's mandrakes." When Jacob approaches, Leah tells him, "You must come in to me; for I have hired you with my son's mandrakes." The use of both of these turns of phrase, coupled with bargaining over a food thought to inspire lust, suggests sex is being traded for the potato roots.[6]

"To make laugh" is slang for intercourse as well. In Genesis 26:6–9, when Isaac and Rebekah travel to Egypt, they stop in Gerar. As with the story of Abraham and Sarah (twice) before, Isaac tells the men who approach them that Rebekah is his sister. After they had been there a "long time," King Abimelech of the Philistines looks out a window and sees Isaac "making Rebekah laugh." The phrase "to make laugh" is a translation of the Hebrew *metsaheq*, which also means "to fondle," used euphemistically here and elsewhere to mean sexual intercourse. Interestingly, the use of *metsaheq* in this passage cleverly refers to Isaac's name, which shares the same *shq* root. Isaac's name was given to him after God told his mother, Sarah, that she would bear a child, making her laugh (Genesis 18:12).

Another story using "to make laugh" is in Genesis 21:9–10. Because of Sarah's inability to produce children for Abraham, she had given him her servant girl Hagar, who ended up giving him his first-born son, Ishmael. After Isaac is born and has been weaned, Abraham throws a great feast to celebrate. While there, "Sarah saw the son of Hagar the Egyptian, whom she had borne to Abraham, making her son Isaac laugh. So she said to Abraham, 'Cast out this slave woman with her son; for the son of this slave woman shall not inherit along with my son Isaac.'" If we read this passage literally, it would seem funny for Sarah to cast out Hagar and Ishmael simply because Ishmael made Isaac laugh. However, if we read it as we read the text in Genesis 26, we see the passage refers to some type of sexual play.[7] Alternatively, some scholars argue that *metsaheq* can also be translated as "to mock with laughter" and that Sarah witnessed Ishmael pretending to be Isaac, the true heir of Abraham.[8] Either interpretation provides enough justification to warrant Sarah's reaction and expulsion of the two.

"Uncovering nakedness" is yet another euphemism for sex. We see this in Leviticus with its list of sexual prohibitions. Leviticus 18:6–7 states, "None of you shall approach anyone near of kin to uncover nakedness ... You shall not uncover the nakedness of your father, which is the nakedness of your mother; she is your mother, you shall not uncover her nakedness." Nakedness can be a term used to refer to genitals, equivalent in meaning and use to the Latin *pudenda*, which means "shame," but which is also the root for *pudendum*, a word used to refer to genitals. Elsewhere in the Bible, such as in Deuteronomy 28:57, Ruth 3:7–14, and Isaiah 7:10, the word "feet" is used as a euphemism for genitals.[9] This may make you rethink how you view the story of Jesus washing his disciples feet in Matthew 26:14 and Luke 22:24.[10]

And while we are touching on the subject, in parallel traditions of the Near East, the word "hand" was often an indirect way to refer to genitals. We see this in a Ugaritic text from the second millennium BCE that reads, "El's hand grows as long as the sea, El's hand [as long as] the ocean."[11] This is the beginning of a narrative describing the conception and birth of the goddesses Dawn and Dusk. El becomes aroused when he sees two women, or two goddesses, and his "hand" grows. We see a similar usage in the Dead Sea Scrolls: "Whoever takes out his hand from under his clothes and his nakedness is seen will be punished for 30 days."[12] Even in the Hebrew Bible, we have an example of "hand" used in place of phallus. At Isaiah 57:8, it reads, "Behind the door and the doorpost you have set up your symbol . . . you have loved their bed, you have gazed on their hand." In other translations, "their phallus" or "their nakedness" is used in place of "their hand."[13] The authors of the Near East's religious texts clearly understood that "hand" was a common term to refer to genitals.

Virginity

Even in the modern world, a tremendous amount of money and energy is spent promoting premarital chastity, particularly for women. This is almost exclusively done in the name of religion. In 1973, R. J. Rushdooney wrote a book titled *The Institutes of Biblical Law*, which championed the philosophy of Dominionism, the idea that Christians should politicize religion. In his book, Rushdooney advocated for the death penalty for, among other things, astrology, incest, adultery, and "unchastity before marriage."[14] The administration of George W. Bush spent one billion dollars on abstinence-only education, which 30 percent of U.S. school systems utilized, and which resulted in a higher rate of teen pregnancy and sexually transmitted diseases.[15] James Dobson, author of *Marriage Under Fire*, an evangelical Christian, and founder of the ferociously anti-gay group Focus on the Family, similarly advocates for abstinence-only sex education.[16] In the 1990s, many religious groups championed the "Allegory of Chastity," a virginity pledge teens took to remain celibate until marriage. This included wearing a silver ring with an inscription of 1 Thessalonians 4:3–4, "For this is the will of God, your sanctification: that you abstain from fornication; that each one of you know how to control your own body in holiness and honor."[17]

So, with all this in mind, what else does the Bible actually say about chastity? Paul of Tarsus provides the clearest references to the matter. The passage of his that has had perhaps the greatest influence on the Church's teachings about celibacy is 1 Corinthians 7:25-26: "Now concerning virgins, I have no command of The Lord, but I give my opinion as one who by the Lord's mercy is trustworthy. I think that, in view of the impending crisis, it is well for you to remain as you are."[18] Though this passage has influenced the Church's views on chastity the most, it is interesting to note that Paul, quite explicitly, states that he is expressing his own personal view and that he is not communicating a command from God or Jesus. What is perhaps even more damning to the Church's reliance on this view is Paul 7:8-9: "To the unmarried and the widows I say that it is well for them to remain unmarried as I am. But if they are not practicing self-control, they should marry. For it is better to marry than to be aflame with passion." In effect, Paul offers an out for those who are not chaste. More significantly, he does not say it is necessary for people to stay celibate—rather, he says that if one were to become "aflame with passion," it would be preferable that one marry.

This is not to say Paul felt premarital sexual activity was okay. He was very much an apocalyptic Jew. He writes in several of his epistles about the "groaning in labor pains" of creation, a metaphor for the coming apocalypse also used in 2 Esdras 4:42, 10:5–14; Matthew 24:8; and Mark 13:8.[19] (Mark 13 predicts a coming apocalypse, often referred to as the "mini apocalypse."[20]) Paul believed that those who were married were more concerned with earthly matters, whereas those who were unmarried and chaste concerned themselves with the desires and needs of God. 1 Corinthians 7:32–34 shows us this:

> *The unmarried man is anxious about the affairs of The Lord, how to please The Lord; but the married man is anxious about the affairs of the world, how to please his wife, and his interests are divided. And the unmarried woman and the virgin are anxious about the affairs of the Lord, so that they may be holy in body and spirit; but the married woman*

is anxious about the affairs of the world, how to please her husband.

This accompanies Paul's aforementioned recommendation to remain celibate and unmarried, like himself, which comes after a number of recommendations in regard to sex. This particular chapter in 1 Corinthians, and the chapters that follow, do focus on sex, but the discussion centers specifically on the eschatological, or apocalyptic, calling from God.[21]

"Eunuch" is another important term to know in the context of the Bible's discussion of sex. While the word means "a man or boy deprived of the testes or external genitals,"[22] for writers of the Bible, it also served as a metaphor for a celibate male. We see this in Matthew 19:12: "For there are eunuchs who have been so from birth, and there are eunuchs who have been made eunuchs by others, and there are eunuchs who have made themselves eunuchs for the sake of the kingdom of heaven. Let anyone accept this who can." Church father Origen took this passage quite literally and castrated himself to avoid sexual temptation.[23] Similar to Paul, Matthew presented celibacy as a way of preparing oneself for the coming kingdom of God during the eschatological age. To be a eunuch, in this sense, was to be celibate voluntarily.

Even the Book of Revelation has an interesting perspective on chastity and virginity. This final book of the New Testament, as an apocalyptic writing, is often equated to the Hebrew Bible's Book of Daniel and makes a rather startling claim in chapter fourteen. It states, "It is these who have not defiled themselves with women, for they are virgins; these follow the Lamb wherever he goes. They have been redeemed from humankind as the first fruits for God and the Lamb." The term "first fruits" in this passage is a call back to Exodus 23:19: "The choicest of the first fruits of your ground you shall bring into the house of the LORD your God." So, it would appear, when the end time comes, these 144,000 virgins (14:1) will be the ones welcomed into God's kingdom. This might explain why, over the course of the two thousand years since the founding of Christianity, only a very small percentage of canonized individuals, whether men or women, had spouses. A very large majority of them were celibate males, with the occasional widow or widower.[24]

Early church fathers like Clement of Alexandria championed Paul of Tarsus' view that marriage was second to chastity.[25] Methodius of Olympus, a Church father and ecclesiastical author, wrote a piece titled *Symposium of the Ten Virgins* (a parody of Plato's *Symposium*) that includes speeches by ten female virgins in praise of chastity. As one virgin argues, procreation may have been absolutely necessary in the beginning, but it has become a "crude and archaic" relic of humanity's origins.[26] In the tenth century, the Church went so far as to attempt to make lay people as chaste as monks, before finally imposing celibacy on clergy in 1215.[27]

Modern-day advocates of premarital celibacy may cite the same Bible passages as their antecedents, but in today's work, the celibate ideal is no longer one that can be reasonably held or expected to be effective.

Polygamy
In 1852, when Brigham Young, the leader of the Mormons after the death of its founder, Joseph Smith, announced

publicly the doctrine of plural marriage, evangelical Christians throughout the United States went into a fury. In response, the U.S. Congress enacted anti-bigamy and anti-polygamy statutes, which in turn were used to prosecute Mormons in federal court. After George Reynolds, a Mormon man with two wives, was tried for his plural marriage, he brought his case to the U.S. Supreme Court, stating that such laws kept him from practicing his religious right to marry several women. The Court, having not yet had the opportunity to clarify the religion clause of the First Amendment, decided unanimously in 1879 that "free religious exercise could not be an excuse to violate the sacred obligation of monogamous marriage by taking on multiple wives." It stated, "Polygamy has always been odious among the northern and western nations of Europe, and, until the establishment of the Mormon Church, was almost exclusively a feature of the life of Asiatic and of African people."[28]

Before the end of the nineteenth century, in a 6–3 ruling, the Supreme Court decided that the Church of Jesus Christ of Latter-day Saints could have its charter of incorporation dissolved and land seized for failing to disavow plural marriage, which the Court saw as "repugnant to public policy" and "a return to barbarism . . . contrary to the spirit of Christianity and of the civilization which Christianity has produced in the Western world." Partisans also took part in state work to see to it that Mormons could not hide behind a claim of religious freedom to continue the practice of polygamy.[29]

These rulings and laws may demonstrate the heartfelt beliefs of American political and judicial figures—as well as the broader American public—but such views toward polygamy are quite contrary to what's actually found in the Bible. As early as Genesis, we see an example of polygamy with Sarah and Abraham at 16:1–4, which touches on the story we explored earlier. Because Sarah is barren, she allows her servant girl, Hagar, to have intercourse with Abraham to ensure he has progeny. According to custom, a woman could take her maid and offer her to the husband and the resulting child would be claimed as the wife's own.[30] Parallels of such an idea are found in other ancient texts. The Code of Hammurapi §146 states: "When a freeman married a priestess and she gave a female slave to her husband and she has then borne children." Similarly, a Nuzi text reads, "If the bride will not bear children, she shall take a woman of the land whence the choicest slaves were obtained as a wife for the bridegroom." And an old Assyrian marriage contract declares, "If within two years she has not procured offspring for him, only she may buy a maid-servant."[31] Similar accounts are seen in Genesis 30:3, with Rachel giving Jacob her maid Bilhah, who gives birth to several sons. A few verses later, Bilhah is no longer able to conceive, so Rachel gives Jacob another slave girl named Zilpah as a wife, and she has children with him as well.

Even after Sarah conceives Isaac, Abraham takes a third wife named Keturah in Genesis 25:1–2. With Keturah, Abraham has the children that eventually start the Arabic tribes of the Midians.[32] Beyond these instances, we also see Esau, Jacob's twin brother who was tricked out of his inheritance, marrying Beeri the Hittite and Basemath in Genesis 26:34. He later takes a daughter of Ishmael, Mahalath, as a third wife in Genesis 28:9.

Outside of Genesis, we see a suggestion of polygamy in 2 Kings 24:15 with King Jehoiachin, who surrenders to the King of Babylon, who in turn took Jehoiachin to Babylon, along with "the king's wives." Jeremiah, in a conversation with Zedekiah, gives a warning at 38:23: "All your wives and your children shall be led out to the Chaldeans, and you yourself shall not escape from their hand . . . this city shall be burned with fire." And in Ezekiel 23:1–4, in a bit of a different situation, two wives of God are mentioned: "they played the whore in Egypt; they played the whore in their youth . . . They became mine and they bore sons and daughters." The names of the two women, Oholibah and Oholah, meant "my tent [is] in her" and "her [own] tent" and referred to Jerusalem and Samaria, respectively, as stated at the end of the fourth verse. Though the passage is a metaphorical one, it suggests the practice of polygamy was unexceptional in the era written.[33]

In ancient Israelite law, we also encounter references that imply the practice of polygamy. For example, Deuteronomy 21:15–17, drawing from Genesis 25:29–34 and the Code of Hammurapi §165–70,[34] says that the children of a less-favored wife are not permitted the father's inheritance. Proverbs 30:21–23, meanwhile, speaks of things that make the earth tremble: "an unloved woman when she gets a husband, and a maid when she succeeds her mistress."

Among the most well-known examples of polygamy in the Bible, there is the story of King David, who had at least eight wives and numerous concubines. We see his wives listed in 1 Samuel 18:27 and 2 Samuel 2:2, 3:2–5, and 11:27. His concubines are mentioned in 2 Samuel 16:21–22 and 1 Kings

1:2–4. Not to be outdone, David's son and the subsequent king of Israel, Solomon, had 700 wives and 300 concubines! This is told to us in 1 Kings 11:3 and the Song of Solomon 6:8.

Men in the Bible derived and communicated power through the practice of polygamy. David took the wives of Saul, the first king of Israel according to the Hebrew Bible, when David became king at 2 Samuel 12:8. When David was dying, his sons competed to be the heir to the throne. We know Solomon won out, but one of David's other sons, Absalom, was bent on taking the throne. He went so far as to "go into" his father's harem in 2 Samuel 16:20–22 to show his claim to the kingship.[35] Absalom is eventually killed by Joab a few chapters later, in 2 Samuel 18:15.

Further, after the Assyrians invaded and defeated Judah at the end of the eighth century BCE, the king of Judah, Hezekiah, had to pay tribute to the king of Assyria, Sennacherib. How did he do it? By giving him his daughters and the palace women. Just as having multiple wives was a sign of power, having few or no wives signaled a lack of power.[36] Furthermore, the wealthier the man, the more partners he could afford, as with King Solomon.

This is not to say that polygamy was not criticized in antiquity. Babylonians and Romans practiced monogamy and spoke out against those of the Jewish faith and the patriarchs who practiced otherwise. During the first century CE, Josephus, who was admittedly polygamous himself, attempted to justify the ten wives of King Herod the Great to Roman antagonists of the practice, saying, "among us it is the custom to have many wives simultaneously."[37]

We have explored a good number of examples in the Bible that endorse polygamy. So, the question then becomes, what was different back then that allowed a culture to embrace and endorse polygamy? Aside from other patriarchal factors, polygamy was practiced for economic purposes—as a means of accruing property. Specifically, when a marriage occurred, the wife was brought into the husband's family along with property from the wife's family.[38] In addition, life expectancy was low, infant mortality rates were high, and women frequently died in child birth. For the society to maintain its population (not even to grow in size), each woman needed to have five children—that is, five *surviving* children. By having multiple wives or concubines, all of whom could share in child rearing, a man also ensured that none of his offspring would be raised without a mother or mother figure. Thus, polygamy served as an institution that helped sustain society's numbers. Because of these facts, polygamous marriage and having concubines made more sense to ensure a man's family line was maintained than being monogamous.[39]

Adultery

Evangelical Christian Pat Robertson has spoken openly about his views that the 9/11 attacks were caused by, among other things, infidelity.[40] Tony Perkins, president of the Family Research Council, an anti-gay marriage and pro-life conservative Christian group, and a former Republican member of the Louisiana House of Representatives, has championed legislation based on or informed by his reading of scripture, including the nation's first "covenant marriage" law. This law made divorce much more difficult in Louisiana.

Subsequently, Arizona and Arkansas adopted similar laws, granting divorce to those in a "covenant marriage" only in cases of physical abuse, imprisonment lasting longer than two years, abandonment, and adultery.[41]

It is because of misinterpreted and misunderstood biblical views on adultery that traditionally only men were allowed into the public forum in the United States and women were expected to stay at home, rear children, and exemplify public morals. In the nineteenth century, the chief justice of the New York Supreme Court, James Kent, went so far as to explain that, because of women's subordination in the Garden of Eden, a male's infidelity did not dissolve a marital contract, as a wife's would. Some jurists took it a step further, saying that the case of a husband committing adultery would not be something the court would waste its time on. Kent said of male adultery, "it is not evidence of such entire depravity, not equally injurious in its effects upon the morals, and good order, and happiness of domestic life," in comparison to a wife's unfaithfulness.[42]

I have mentioned that these rules and ideas, perpetuated by more recent laws, are misinformed; they are nothing more than enforced propaganda written by and for men in a patriarchal society. The original meaning behind prohibitions against infidelity is lost on contemporary society. When the Bible was written, the act of adultery was specific to a man having intercourse with a woman married to another man. Such an act was seen, in essence, as the expropriation of property by the man engaging in the act. We can see this in the Ten Commandments. Exodus 20:14 may read, "You shall not commit adultery," which sounds universal in nature, but looking at the gender of the individuals addressed in the rest of the Ten Commandments, we see that this line very specifically refers to a man committing adultery with a woman—a married woman.[43] This same passage is shared in Deuteronomy 5:18, where the Decalogue is repeated. Parallels are seen in Leviticus 20:10, which apportions blame to both the man and the woman: "If a man commits adultery with the wife of his neighbor, both the adulterer and the adulteress shall be put to death." Deuteronomy 22:22 similarly states, "If a man is caught lying with the wife of another man, both of them shall die, the man who lay with the woman as well as the woman. So you shall purge the evil from Israel."

Contrary to the laws laid out in the Pentateuch, other ancient Near Eastern laws, such as the Code of Hammurapi §129, did not require the death of the woman in such situations—or, at least, the decision was left up to the husband. In this regard, the people of Israel made the woman responsible, or at least partially responsible, for her actions in cases of adultery.[44] These laws and prohibitions turned adultery from merely a breach of contract between couples to a slight against the God of Israel and the community as a whole. Of significant note, they also gave the woman the status of being a legal person.[45] In effect, the price a woman paid for being treated as a legal person in this context was death.[46] Also of significant note, a married man did not commit adultery if he slept with a woman who was not married, promised, betrothed, or engaged to another man, since no one else's (read: no other *man's*) rights were being violated.

In the New Testament—specifically, in the Gospel of Matthew 5:27–30—Jesus offers additional amendments to the Israelite laws, including equating anger toward another to murder and swearing to Jerusalem, the earth, or by heaven to swearing to God. Jesus tells us, in the passage at hand, not only that committing adultery is bad but also that "everyone that looks *at a woman* with lust has already committed adultery with *her* in *his* heart [emphasis my own]." Again, these proscriptions are targeted at men. It is difficult to look at the this passage, with its gender-specific pronouns, and argue it is addressing women. These are laws by men, for men.

Aside from specific laws speaking out against adultery and infidelity, the Bible also details adulterous behavior. The most notable instance occurs with King David and Bathsheba in 2 Samuel 11:1–4. David, while atop the roof of his home, sees Bathsheba bathing and finds her to be very beautiful. He sends someone to find out who she is and discovers she is not only the daughter of Eliam and son of Ahithophem, David's adviser, but also the wife of Uriah the Hittite, one of David's thirty best soldiers (2 Samuel 23:39). This revelation does not seem to bother him, as he then sends messengers to get her. She arrives, and "he lay with her."

Problems arise for David when, a verse later, Bathsheba tells David that she is pregnant. David comes up with a plan and requests Joab to bring Uriah home from battle in order to have him sleep with Bathsheba and cover up the infidelity. When Uriah arrives, David plays it cool, asking how Joab and the people are doing and about the war. Then, he tells Uriah to go home and "wash his feet"—a euphemism, as you will recall, for sex—with Bathsheba. However, because the Israelites were at the time involved in a holy war—"The ark and Israel and Judah remain at Succoth" (2 Samuel 11:11)—

Uriah, a pious, consecrated soldier, refuses to have intercourse with her, likely because ejaculation, according to Leviticus 15, would have made him impure for a day. Even after David gets Uriah drunk, Uriah refuses to have intercourse with his wife (verses 9–13). As a result, David ends up sending Uriah to the frontlines, where he is killed (11:14–17). Quite the guy, that King David. It does come back to bite him, though. In 2 Samuel 12, David's son is punished with death for David's sins, contrary to what Ezekiel 8:19–20 states as being fair,

Yet you say, "Why should not the son suffer for the iniquity of the father?" When the son has done what is lawful and right, and has been careful to observe all my statutes, he shall surely live. The person who sins shall die. A child shall not suffer for the iniquity of a parent, nor a parent suffer for the iniquity of a child; the righteousness of the righteous shall be his own, and the wickedness of the wicked shall be his own.

But what about Jesus? Did he say anything about adultery and how to follow the law? In the Book of John 8:1–11, we have a story where Jesus faces a woman charged with adultery. Let us forget for a moment that it is only the woman who is brought before Jesus and the man is absent or excused from punishment and that this story is missing from the earliest copies of John's manuscript available to us.[47] But in this story, Jesus is told that, according to the law, the woman should be put to death. Jesus responds, "Let he who is without sin cast the first stone," and the angry mob disperses. When Jesus asks the woman if they condemn her, she says no, and Jesus responds, "Neither do I condemn you. Go your way, and from now on do not sin again." I think it is safe to say that, for anyone who accepts that this is the written word of God and that Jesus actually said this, then we can just ignore the rest of the Bible's prohibitions against sexual activity. If Jesus does not listen to the law, then why should anyone else?[48]

Incest

Incest, sex between two closely related family members, is certainly frowned upon in the United States. Depending on the state that you reside in, or where the offense occurs, you can receive a penalty ranging anywhere from five years (Hawaii, Florida) to life imprisonment (Georgia, the Carolinas, Tennessee, Alabama, Louisiana, and Mississippi) for sex with a linear ancestor (parent, grandparent, child, grandchild). Other states, like Ohio, apply the law only to parent-child relationships, while New Jersey does not impose a penalty if both parties are over eighteen.[49] Some states even forbid sex between family members who are not related by blood, such as between a step-parent and step-child.[50]

Laws related to marriage, cohabitation, and sexual relations between first cousins vary about as widely as the linear incest laws, but first cousins are allowed to marry in about twenty states. A few states, such as Arizona and Illinois,[51] permit such relationships as long as one of the partners is infertile or sterile.

The issue of incest invariably comes up when abortion is debated, with many anti-abortion proponents saying that abortion should be illegal even in cases of incest. For example, Republican Virginia state representative Bob Marshall argued in early 2014 that, according to the Bible, incest is voluntary and thus incest should not be a considered an exception in abortion cases. This is also the same person who, at a rally to defund Planned Parenthood, said any woman who has an abortion will birth disabled children in subsequent pregnancies. He also accused U.S. Supreme Court Justice Anthony Kennedy of being gay after writing the majority response that struck down the Defense of Marriage Act and California's Proposition 8.[52]

I am against incest for various reasons and am thus not arguing for a positive position for incest here; rather, I'm trying to demonstrate once again how often laws are based on (often selective) biblical literalism.[53] Adultery and the subject of incest often occur together in the Bible. For example, Deuteronomy 27:20 refers to someone sleeping with his father's wife. A similar, almost verbatim passage is found at Deuteronomy 22:30, which says a man must not marry his father's wife. Doing so would "uncover his father's skirt"— as it reads in a direct translation from Hebrew—and violate his father's rights. The act would also bring into question the paternity of any children birthed by the father's wife.

In a long passage, Leviticus 18:6–16 talks about interfamily relations and prohibitions against them. "None of you shall approach anyone near of kin to uncover nakedness . . . of your father, which is the nakedness of your mother . . . of your father's wife . . . of your sister, your father's daughter or your mother's daughter." The prohibitions continue against uncovering the nakedness of one's grandchildren, half- or step-siblings, sisters, aunts, uncles, daughters-in-law, and brothers' wives. Again, the prohibitions are very male-oriented.

Notably, there is no prohibition against a father sleeping with his daughter. Again, this ties in with the prohibitions of adultery; there is a bride price with marriage, and marriage contracts. Prior to marriage, a woman is the property of her father. We see evidence of this in Exodus 21:7, "When a man sells his daughter as a slave, she shall not go out as the male slaves do." Ensuing verses refer to the woman's husband as "her master."[54] These writings are by men, for men.

Given the prohibitions and laws surrounding incest, it is interesting to consider the various cases of incest in the Bible. We see more than one example in the very first book. Incest may be prohibited according to Leviticus, but no one told Abraham, the great patriarch of not only Christianity but also of Judaism and Islam, who is guilty of incest! In Genesis 20:12–13, it is revealed that Sarah, Abraham's first wife, is "indeed my sister, the daughter of my father but not the daughter of my mother, and she became my wife . . . I said to her, 'This is the kindness you must do me: at every place to which we come, say of me, He is my brother.'" So, when Abraham tells people that Sarah is his sister, he is not lying. Sarah is his father's daughter.

If we look back to Genesis 11:26–29, we can see that Abraham's family does, indeed, like to keep it in the family. We learn Abraham's father, Thare, has three sons. Those sons are Abram (who later becomes Abraham), Nachor, and Aran. The end of the passage in question reads, ". . . and the name of Nachor's wife, Melcha, the *daughter of Aran* [emphasis my own]"—meaning Nachor marries the daughter of Aran, the third brother.

But it does not stop there for Abraham's family. After the destruction of Sodom and Gomorrah, Abraham's nephew, Lot, escapes with his family, only to have his wife turn into a pillar of salt for disobeying God and looking back at the cities during their destruction. After some time has passed, in Genesis 19:31–36, Lot's two daughters discuss their belief that there is no one left out there in the world. "'Our father is old, and there is no man left on the earth to come in to us after the manner of the whole earth. Come, let us make him drunk with wine, and let us lie with him, that we may preserve the seed of our father.'" So, for two consecutive nights, Lot's daughters get him drunk, have intercourse with him, and become "with child by their father."

In another case of incest in Genesis, Tamar, knowing she is viewed as "damaged goods" following the death of her husband and her husband's brother, Onan, for failing to conceive, dresses as a prostitute. Her father-in-law, not recognizing her, approaches and says, "Come, let me come in to you" (Genesis 38:16), impregnating her with twins.

It is not solely in Genesis that we see incestuous stories. Exodus 6:19–20 reads, "And Amram took to wife Jochabed his aunt by the father's side: and she bore him Aaron and Moses." Take a minute to think about this: two of the central figures to the Exodus story, patriarchs of the Judeo-Christian faith, were born out of an intrafamilial relationship. Moses, the man who God called upon to lead the Israelites out of Egypt and whose legend was the inspiration for some aspects of Jesus' life and ministry, had parents who were relatives.

Other accounts of incest include the story of Amnon and Thamar (2 Kings 13:8-14), though that is an account of rape that is already understood to be wrong and that Thamar's brother, Absalom, makes right by killing Amnon. There is also the question of how Cain, of Cain and Abel infamy, was able to find a wife when his parents were the only two people alive before him (4:16–17). But these stories emphasize the point that, even with prohibitions against such sexual practices, cases of them exist in the Bible, sometimes involving leading biblical figures.

Indeed, the Bible provides exceptions to the prohibitions against certain forms of incest. The story of Onan in Genesis (38:8–10), for example, illustrates what is called a levirate marriage. The laws for such a marriage are laid out in Deuteronomy 25:5–10, but the general gist is, if a husband dies and leaves no male heirs, the wife "shall not marry outside of the family to a stranger." This meant that the next brother would have intercourse with the dead brother's wife to ensure she became pregnant and had a child. This, again, goes back to the concept of paying a bride price. In turn, any son thus conceived was considered the son of the deceased brother. Disobeying this law, Onan pulled out and "spilled his seed whenever he went in to his brother's wife," for which God killed him.

In certain circumstances, some prohibitions, like child sacrifice and bestiality (Leviticus 18:21, 23), were mentioned because they were practiced by other Near Eastern religions.[55] However, rules against incest seem nearly universal, even in the ancient world. In the Code of Hammurapi §154, for example, it states that men who have sex with their daughters must leave the city. Other Babylonian laws involving incest, or sexual impropriety, such as a man sleeping with a woman betrothed to his son (§155), imply that it is the man and not the woman who is guilty in such a situation. (Recall how the Israelites made a woman legally responsible for her adulterous actions.) The Hittite's had laws that clearly mirror the Israelite laws in Leviticus. On the second law tablet, §189 prohibits intercourse with one's mother, daughter, and son, §190 with one's stepmother while the stepfather is still alive, and §195 with one's brother's wife while the brother is alive, while §193 suggests a levirate marriage, also allowed in Middle Assyrian law, if the brother dies.[56]

Cultural and religious prohibitions against incest exist for good reasons. In a recent case coming out of Australia, an incest "cult" had sexual free-for-alls over the course of four generations. The children who resulted had multiple disabilities, including walking impairments and hearing and sight problems. One boy, for example, had eyes that were misaligned.[57] In a study of Czechoslovakian children with parents who were first-degree relatives, 42 percent were born with severe birth defects or suffered an early death, and an additional 11 percent had mild mental handicaps. By comparison, a control group whose parents were not related had a 7 percent chance of having a birth defect. The science seems to indicate pretty clearly that incest does bad things for a species.[58]

Bestiality

The United States currently has no federal laws against bestiality, or zoophilia, practiced by an adult. Such laws are determined by the state, though when children are involved federal law does take effect.[59] There are only twelve U.S. states that have no laws regarding bestiality, with seventeen states classifying bestiality as a felony and eighteen as a misdemeanor. The military also has rules against it. On May

31, 1951, Harry S Truman signed into law the Uniform Code of Military Justice (UCMJ), which, in article 125, states, "any person subject to this chapter who engages in unnatural carnal copulation . . . with an animal is guilty of sodomy. Penetration, however slight, is sufficient to complete the offense."[60] This article was repealed, at least in relation to the comparison to sodomy, but the code still emphasized that bestiality warranted a punishment "as a court-martial may direct."[61]

Family Research Council president Tony Perkins was outraged in 2011 when, for a brief time, bestiality was taken out of the UCMJ, along with sodomy and adultery laws. "It's all about using the military to advance this administration's radical social agenda," he said. "Not only did they overturn Don't Ask Don't Tell, but they had another problem, and that is, under military law, sodomy is illegal, just as adultery is illegal, so they had to remove that prohibition against sodomy . . . the House will have problems with this bill."[62] What this quotation demonstrates above anything else is that bestiality is often equated with homosexuality. Indeed, in Leviticus 18:22–23, the prohibition against male-on-male intercourse is closely followed by a law against bestiality. "You shall not have sexual relations with any animal and defile yourself with it, nor shall any woman give herself to an animal to have sexual relations with it: it is perversion."

Here it is important to note that, just as the Israelites did not want to physically mix with the Canaanites, they also did not want to mix their cultural practices with the practices of other cultures. The ancient Israelites viewed any such act of mixing as unnatural. This explains why there is a prohibition against wearing clothes with mixed fibers, the mating of two different animal species, and the planting of two different kinds of seed in the same bed (Leviticus 19:19). Mixing their culture with the Canaanites was just as unnatural to the Israelites as mixing animal breeds, fibers in cloth, and seeds in soil—and, by extension, bestiality and homosexuality. The Israelites did not want intercultural mixing of any kind.[63]

The prohibition of bestiality was also based on a fear of crossing the boundary between what was viewed as natural and unnatural—that which separates man and animal. Given the Genesis creation story, which championed man as having dominion over the animals, it would be completely unnatural to allow people to have intercourse with animals. Additional prohibitions against bestiality are found in Exodus (22:19) and Deuteronomy (27:21).

One thing that is important to note is that, in the context of the Bible, none of the prohibitions mentioned in this section stand out as being more important than the others. Unlike what modern moralizers will say, bestiality in the Bible is not any more of a stronger offense than participating in male-on-male penetration or mixing crops or fibers. This is not to say bestiality should be legal, as there are many reasons bestiality should be illegal based on secular ethics. Rather, this is to make clear that, when moralizers point to the Bible to decry bestiality while wearing a cotton and wool blend, they yet again are doing nothing more than practicing selective biblical literalism.[64]

Prostitution and Orgies

Prostitution in the United States is illegal, with the exception of a few counties in Nevada, which collectively have a couple dozen legal brothels. It was legal in Rhode Island between 1980 and 2009, when Governor Donald Carcieri signed into law a bill that made the purchase and sale of sex illegal.[65] In Louisiana, convicted prostitutes must register as a sex offender, while those caught paying for sex are not required to do so.[66]

Prostitutes represent an incredibly small group among the U.S. population—23 out of every 100,000 people.[67] However, the rate of death among active prostitutes is 5.9 times higher than that of the general population. It is triple the rate of the fishing profession, which the U.S. Bureau of Labor Statistics cites as having the highest fatality rate among any (legal) profession.[68]

An article titled "A Biblical Perspective on Prostitution" on the Life Ministries website gives a rather clear idea why those who wish to legalize prostitution in the United States and elsewhere in the world face an uphill battle against religious moralizers.[69] It cites scripture like Leviticus 19:29, "Do not degrade your daughter by making her a prostitute." In effect, according to this verse, being a prostitute is degrading, but being the property of another person with the power to "make" you something is not. Interesting. And let's not forget the other prohibitions we find right before this in Leviticus— prohibitions against marking the skin (tattoos), practicing witchcraft, and shaving one's face.

Life Ministries also cites Leviticus 21:9, which mentions prostitution carried out by the daughter of a priest. The punishment for such a crime? Burning the daughter to death. Chances are, if such a law was written specifically about the daughters of priests, then they were likely prostituting themselves enough to have been noticed and to cause a bit of a stir with the Israelites. In truth, cultic prostitution was very much commonplace in the ancient world.[70] Herodotus, a historian from the fifth century BCE, wrote of the societies along the Tigris and Euphrates and their temples where women performed sacred prostitution as a form of worship to the gods,

> *The foulest Babylonian custom is that which compels every woman of the land to sit in the temple of Aphrodite and have intercourse with some stranger once in her life . . . Once a woman has taken her place there, she does not go away to her home before some stranger has cast money into her lap, and had intercourse with her outside the temple; but while he casts the money, he must say, "I invite you in the name of Mylitta [the Assyrian name for Aphrodite]."*[71]

Other sections of the Hebrew Bible reference prostitution pejoratively, without expressly forbidding it. Proverbs 7:10 speaks of a woman *dressed* as a prostitute in a verse about adultery.[72] Jeremiah 3:3 mentions someone having the "forehead of a whore"—"forehead" here meaning "stubbornness."[73] But positive references to prostitutes also exist in the Bible. For example, in Joshua 2, two spies sent by Joshua to Jericho stay with a prostitute who hides them when the king of Jericho sends out men to intercept them. There is even a suggestion that Jesus hung out with prostitutes, but that view is hard to justify based only on scripture. In Luke 7:37, a "sinful" woman anoints Jesus with oil, but "sinful" does not necessarily mean she was a "prostitute." Indeed, this story is paralleled in Mark 14:3–9 and Matthew 26:6–13, and those two earlier accounts do not say anything about the woman being sinful. And in John 12:1-8, after the resurrection of Lazarus, it is one of Lazarus' sisters who anoints Jesus with oil, with no mention of sin, let alone prostitution.

Hosea 4:11–19 provides clear evidence that other Near Eastern cultures practiced ritual prostitution. It mentions those who devote themselves to "whoredom" and who provide oracles by speaking to "a piece of wood" and a "divining rod." The reference to "wood" suggests the Canaanite goddess known as Asherah, a fertility deity. A direct reference to temple prostitutes comes at the very end of verse 14, ". . . for the men go aside with whores, and sacrifice with temple prostitutes; thus a people without understanding comes to ruin."[74]

In the Book of Ezekiel, we find a description of temple prostitution occurring within the Temple of Jerusalem—Solomon's Temple. Ezekiel 8:2–18 describes visions of idolatry in the temple. At verse 5, Ezekiel describes "this image of jealousy." As in Hosea, this reference likely refers to the goddess Asherah. We know from 2 Kings 21:7 that King Manasseh had put a pole honoring her in the Temple. At verses 14–15, we see women weeping for "Tammuz," a Mesopotamian god. In verses 16–18, Ezekiel describes a "climactic abomination," which refers to Sun worship, as verified by 2 Kings 23:5,11 and an Israelite ritual stand in Taanach that shows the sun deity. The combination of the goddess Asherah and the women weeping in the Temple suggest the presence of temple prostitutes employed for the worship of pagan Near Eastern gods.[75] We see a very explicit example of them in 2 Kings 23:4–7, when images made for pagan gods are brought out of the Temple and destroyed, as are the ritual booths of the male temple prostitutes where the women did "weaving for Asherah."

Now, in regard to orgies, I touch on the subject briefly because the Bible does indeed make reference to them. At Galatians 5:21, Paul writes, "drunkenness, orgies, and the like. I warn you, as I did before, that those who live like this will not inherit the kingdom of God." His intentions with this line are very similar to the early Israelites' intentions with Leviticus—namely, to prevent foreign cultural practices from mixing with Israelite culture. In this instance, these included the Greco-Roman practices to which verses 19–23 refer. Similar xenophobic ideas are seen in Mark 7:21–22, Romans 1:29–31, and 1 Corinthians 6:9–10, among many others.

Conclusion

As demonstrated, there is a lot to consider and detail when tracing the roots of sex-based laws and sexual taboos in the modern world. We have seen laws that stem from biological instincts and urges—things that are ingrained in us naturally that people of antiquity sought to put on the lips of their deity to make sense of them. But we have also seen biblical laws that stem from a desire to dissuade followers of the Israelite, Jewish, and eventual Christian faith from participating in the practices of other cultures. As a result, much of modern law related to sex is based in large part on a faulty foundation, as political leaders justify legislation by citing a book that is often untethered to sexual and physical realities—and that often offers conflicting messages about what is and is not permissible, particularly when considering the exceptions granted to many of the most well-known biblical figures.

Notes

1.   "Backseat bingo" is a term from the 1950s for passionate kissing or necking in the backseat of a car. See Urban Dictionary, http://www.urbandictionary.com/define.php?term=backseat%20 bingo (last accessed December 27, 2014).

2.   David M. Carr, "Genesis," in *The New Oxford Annotated Bible* (New York: Oxford University Press, 2010), 16–17.

3.   Michael Coogan, *God and Sex: What the Bible Really Says* (New York: Grand Central Publishing, 2010), 13/168, iBooks edition.

4.   Bernard M. Levinson, "Deuteronomy," in *The New Oxford Annotated Bible* (New York: Oxford University Press, 2010), 284.

5.   K. Lawson Younger, Jr., "Joshua," in *The New Oxford Annotated Bible* (New York: Oxford University Press, 2010), 323.

6.   Carr, *Annotated*, 52–53.

7.   Victor P. Hamilton, *The New International Commentary on the Old Testament: The Book of Genesis: Chapters 18–50* (Grand Rapids: William B. Eerdmans Publishing Company, 1995), 79.

8.   Robert Alter, *The Five Books of Moses* (New York: W. W. Norton & Company, 2004), 103.

9.   Coogan, *God and Sex*, 77.

10.   Jeffrey Stackert, "Leviticus," in *The New Oxford Annotated Bible* (New York: Oxford University Press, 2010), 169.

11.   Ugarit is in the northern part of what is now Syria.

12.   In a document titled "Rules of the Community" at 1QSm column seven, lines 13–14, as cited in Coogan, *God and Sex*, 17.

13.   Marvin A. Sweeney, "Isaiah," in *The New Oxford Annotated Bible* (New York: Oxford University Press, 2010), 1044.

14.   Chris Hedges, *American Fascists: The Christian Right and the War on America* (New York: 2006), 11–13.

15. Hedges, *Fascists*, 24.

16. Hedges, *Fascists*, 84–85.

17. Jonathan Haidt, *The Righteous Mind: Why Good People Are Divided by Politics and Religion* (New York: Pantheon Books, 2012), 174.

18. As argued and cited in Coogan, *God and Sex*, 30.

19. Neil Elliot, "Romans," in *The New Oxford Annotated Bible* (New York: Oxford University Press, 2010), 1987.

20. Bart D. Ehrman, *The New Testament: A Historical Introduction to the Early Christian Writings*, 4th ed. (New York: Oxford University Press, 2008), 85.

21. Laurence L. Welborn, "The First Letter of Paul to the Corinthians," in *The New Oxford Annotated Bible* (New York: Oxford University Press, 2010), 2007-8.

22. Dictionary.com, http://dictionary.reference.com/browse/eunuch (last accessed August 17, 2014).

23. John Boswell, *Christianity, Social Tolerance, and Homosexuality* (Chicago: University of Chicago Press, 1980), 98.

24. Coogan, *God and Sex*, 31.

25. Elaine Pagels, *Adam, Eve, and the Serpent* (New York: Random House, 1988), 28.

26. As quoted in Pagels, *Serpent*, 85.

27. Karen Armstrong, *Holy War: The Crusades and Their Impact on Today's World* (New York: Anchor Books, 2001), 56, 229.

28. As quoted in David Sehat, *The Myth of American Religious Freedom* (New York: Oxford University Press, 2011), 169–71.

29. Sehat, *Myth*, 172.

30. Carr, *Annotated*, 33.

31. Victor P. Hamilton, *The New International Commentary on the Old Testament: the Book of Genesis: Chapters 1–17* (Grand Rapids:

William B, Eerdmans Publishing Company, 1990), 444.

32. Carr, *Annotated*, 45.

33. Stephen L. Cook, "Ezekiel," in *The New Oxford Annotated Bible* (New York: Oxford University Press, 2010), 1191.

34. Levinson, *Annotated*, 285.

35. Steven L. McKenzie, "2 Samuel," in *The New Oxford Annotated Bible* (New York: Oxford University Press, 2010), 469.

36. Coogan, *God and Sex*, 60.

37. Pagels, *Serpent*, 11.

38. Michael Coogan, *The Old Testament: A Historical Introduction to the Hebrew Scriptures* (New York: Oxford University Press, 2011), 85.

39. Shawna Dolansky and Richard Elliot Friedman, *The Bible Now* (New York: Oxford University Press, 2011), 28, Kindle edition.

40. Hedges, *Fascists*, 109.

41. Hedges, *Fascists*, 138.

42. Sehat, *Myth*, 104.

43. Carol Meyers, "Exodus," in *The New Oxford Annotated Bible* (New York: Oxford University Press, 2010), 111.

44. Levinson, *Annotated*, 286.

45. Levinson, *Annotated*, 260–61.

46. Martti Nissinen, *Homoeroticism in the Biblical World: A Historical Perspective* (Minneapolis: Fortress Press, 1998), 63.

47. Jerome H. Neyrey, "John," in *The New Oxford Annotated Bible* (New York: Oxford University Press, 2010), 1895.

48. Coogan, *God and Sex*, 96.

49. "Inbred Obscurity: Improving Incest Laws in the Shadow of the 'Sexual Family,'" *Harvard Law Review* 119, no. 8 (2006): 2464–2485.

50. Jeffrey S. Turner, *Encyclopedia of Relationships across the Lifespan* (Westport: Greenwood Publishing Group, 1996), 92.

51. See Arizona's A.R.S. §25–10 (2010) and Illinois' §750 ILCS 5/212 (2010).

52. "Republican House Candidate Says Incest Exemptions in Abortion Laws Are Unnecessary," *Politicus USA*, April 13, 2014, http://tinyurl.com/kdlcyx7 (accessed December 26, 2014).

53. See Kent Greenawalt, *Religion and the Constitution: Volume 2: Establishment and Fairness* (Princeton: Princeton University Press, 2009), 529.

54. Meyers, *Annotated*, 112.

55. Stackert, *Annotated*, 170.

56. Jonathan R. Ziskind, "Legal Rules of Incest in the Ancient Near East," RIDA 35 (1988): 80–87, available at http://tinyurl.com/ny8yf3n.

57. Richard Shears, "Ragtag Children of Horrifying Incest 'Cult' Found Living Deformed, Filthy and Mute in Scenic Australian Valley Spent Their Days Having Sex and Cutting Animals' Genitals," *Daily Mail*, December 2, 2013, http://tinyurl.com/oujvz3n.

58. Hal Herzog, "The Problem with Incest: Evolution, Morality, and the Politics of Abortion," *Huffington Post*, October 9, 2012, http://tinyurl.com/o6ka862.

59. "Zoophilia and the Law—Laws around the World Affecting Zoophiles," Lectric Law Library, http://www.lectlaw.com/files/sex13.htm (accessed August 20, 2014).

60. "Key Dates in U.S. Policy on Gay Men and Women in Military Service," U.S. Naval Institute, 2014, http://m.usni.org/news-and-features/dont-ask-dont-tell/timeline (accessed August 20, 2014).

61. 10 U.S. Code §925—Article 125. Forcible sodomy; bestiality (1950), http://www.law.cornell.edu/uscode/text/10/925.

62. Pete Winn, "Senate Approves Bill that Legalizes Sodomy and Bestiality in U.S. Military," *cnsnews.com*, December 1, 2011, http://tinyurl.comnejb93r.

63. Coogan, *God and Sex,* 82.

64. Coogan, *God and Sex*, 82.

65. Lynn Arditi, "Bill Signing Finally Outlaws Indoor Prostitution in R.I.," *Providence Journal*, November 3, 2009, http://cdn.ca9.uscourts.gov/datastore/library/2013/02/26/Coyote_prostitution.pdf.

66. Nathan Koppel, "Louisiana's 'Crime Against Nature' Sex Law Draws Legal Fire," *Wall Street Journal*, February 16, 2011, http://tinyurl.com/oexh2hs.

67. J. J. Potterat, D. E. Woodhouse, J. B. Muth, and S. Q. Muth, "Prostitution and the Sex Discrepancy in Reported Number of Sexual Partners," *Proceedings of the National Academy of Sciences* (1990): 233–43.

68. J. J. Potterat, D. D. Brewer, S. Q. Muth, R. B. Rothenberg, D. E. Woodhouse, J. B. Muth, H. K. Stites, and S. Brody, "Mortality in a Long-Term Open Cohort of Prostitute Women," *American Journal of Epidemiology* (2004): 778–85.

69. Anderson Lansdown, "A Biblical Perspective on Prostitution," Life Ministries, http://www.lifeministries.org.au/pamphlets.php?content_id=53 (accessed December 26, 2014).

70. Wenham, *Commentary*, 291.

71. Herodotus, *The Histories* 1.199, trans. George Rawlinson (South Australia: Adelaide University Press, 2014), https://ebooks.adelaide.edu.au/h/herodotus/h4/book1.html.

72. Katherine Dell, "Proverbs," in *The New Oxford Annotated Bible* (New York: Oxford University Press, 2010), 904.

73. Rodney R. Hutton, "Jeremiah," in *The New Oxford Annotated Bible* (New York: Oxford University Press, 2010), 1063.

74. Gregory Mobley, "Hosea," in *The New Oxford Annotated Bible* (New York: Oxford University Press, 2010), 1264.

75. Cook, *Annotated*, 1170–71.

2

Women

Women are at a pretty unfair disadvantage in the United States. The National Committee on Pay Equity estimates that women earn only 76.5 percent of what men earned for the same amount of work. And it only gets worse for most women of color: Asian American women make 92 percent, but Latinas and African American women make 57.5 percent and 68.6 percent, respectively. Fields often considered "women's work," such as nursing and teaching, are among the lowest paid jobs in the work force.[1] While the oft-stated statistic that women perform two-thirds of the world's work, receive only 10 percent of the world's income, and own only 1 percent of the world's means of production is likely faulty,[2] the fact that women are treated as second-class citizens throughout much of the world is unassailable. Forms of oppression manifest in manifold ways, including through physical violence. According to the Rape, Abuse & Incest National Network (RAINN), for example, one of every six American women has been a victim of a completed or attempted rape, and 90 percent of rape victims are female. Further, an estimated seventeen to eighteen million American women have been victims of rape or sexual assault.[3]

What Does the Bible Say?

Justification for treating women as second-class citizens, or at least the excuse for doing so, starts very early on. Genesis 2:23–24 says, "Then the man said, 'This at last is bone of my bones and flesh of my flesh; this one shall be called Woman, for out of Man this one was taken.' Therefore a man leaves his father and his mother and clings to his wife, and they become one flesh." This very passage became the inspiration for Jewish marriage and sex laws in the first century CE.[4] It was believed that intercourse between a man and woman demonstrated the connection that God created in the beginning between humans.[5]

Further, Genesis 3:16 reads, "To the woman he said, 'I will greatly increase your pangs in childbearing; in pain you shall bring forth children, yet your desire shall be for your husband, and he shall rule over you." A disintegration of the relationship and connectedness they originally had is likely what was originally implied,[6] but the issue with using this passage, for the purpose of denigrating women, is that this passage was not intended, nor is it laid out, as a command from God. This passage, the creation story, is actually what is known as an etiology. It is an explanation for the origins of, or reason for, circumstances in the world around us. Why do snakes have no legs? Because of the serpent's deceit in Eden. Why do women have labor pains? Because of Eve's decision to eat the fruit, as God commanded her and Adam not to do. Why is the soil of the earth hard to work with to produce food? Because of man's fall in the Garden. Similarly, a woman *is* submissive to her husband because of the story of Adam and Eve. This is an origin story; as such, it does not equate to a prescription. Nowhere in Genesis does it require or command that a woman *should* submit to her husband.[7]

Lastly, the Genesis creation story refers to God creating a "helper" in 2:18. The Hebrew used here, *'ezer kenegedo*, translates as either "suitable helper" or "help meet." It can also mean "strength" and, given the context, would translate as "a strength corresponding to him." So the story, in its native language, suggests not a person made inferior to her male counterpart, but someone of equal status. More notably, this same Hebrew term is used to refer to the Israelite God numerous times, such as in Psalm 121:2, 124:8, 146:5, 33:20, 115:9–11; Exodus 18:4; and Deuteronomy 33:72.[8] So, if we cite Genesis to argue that women are inferior to men, then we must also reason that God is inferior to men, because the same title is given to God. Truthfully, even the most devout should not cite Genesis to say women are inferior to men, because the context does not suggest this.

But what about other sections of the Bible? In the New Testament, in the writings of Paul, we see at 1 Corinthians 11:3, "But I want you to understand that Christ is the head of every man, and man is the head of the woman, and God is the head of Christ." What is problematic here, looking at this line within the context of the letter as a whole, is Paul's mixed messages. For example, in chapter 14, he talks of women participating in important acts of church leadership, such as with prophesying, while also calling on women to remain silent in church (14:33–36). These contradictions may partly be due to later insertions. For example, some consider 11:3 ("The head of the woman is man") to be a later insertion. Either way, within the context of the letter, it is hard to balance these two clearly opposing views of women—both having a prominent place among men in the Corinthian church and being told to be subservient and quiet.[9]

There are other epistles by Paul that mention a hierarchy between men and women. We can see these in the first letter to Timothy, which, by all accounts, is a pseudonymous letter written to sound like Paul. The style of writing, theology, and vocabulary all indicate it is likely a member of one of the churches he founded wrote it.[10] In the first letter to Timothy, the author writes at 2:11–15, "Let a woman learn in silence with full submission. I permit no woman to teach or to have authority over a man ... For Adam was formed first, then Eve ...Yet she will be saved through childbearing." This lays out a clear indication that this letter was likely not written by Paul, because if we look at his epistle to the Romans, a letter thought to be a genuine letter of Paul, Paul actually emphasizes in 5:12–21 that it is Adam who caused the transgression that put sin on humanity for Jesus to come and correct. As he states in Romans 5:18–19, "Therefore just as one man's trespass led to condemnation for all, so one man's act of righteousness leads to justification and life for all. For just as by the one man's disobedience the many were made sinners, so by the one man's obedience the many will be made righteous." So, there is an unexplained contradiction here if we take the view that both of these two letters were written by Paul. As with sections of 1 Corinthians, this suggests a later author did the writing.[11]

There is also a mention of women being submissive to their husbands in 1 Peter 3:1, "Wives, in the same way, accept the authority of your husbands, so that, even if some of them do not obey the word, they may be won over without a word by their wives' conduct." This is all well and good, but we have a similar problem here. First, we have an account in Acts that says Peter, the right-hand man to Jesus and alleged founder of the Church, is uneducated and illiterate. Acts 4:13 reads, "Now when they saw the boldness of Peter and John and realized that they were uneducated and ordinary men, they were amazed and recognized them as companions of Jesus." We also know he was pretty uneducated because he was a fisherman in Galilee, a job that required no education. The language and wording of the Septuagint, the Greek translation of the Hebrew Bible, in 1 Peter, as well as the clearly competent, knowledgeable notation, is also a fairly clear indicator the author was not Peter, as his native tongue was Aramaic. Collectively, these facts, coupled with the numerous gospels, "Acts" of Peter, and Apocalypses of Peter in circulation during the first and second century, make it likely that the letter was written by a later author in Peter's name.[12]

If people read these verses as representing God's word, then they are taking it from a writer who intentionally wrote to deceive and who wanted to push his own agenda over the writings of a legitimate Church leader who advocated for women having an equal role in the church. At the very least, people willing to take these verses as the word of God, or a command from God, have to accept they were passed along through deceit and contradict other parts of canonical writings that advocate for equality—at least as much equality as first-century writings in the Near East would allow.

Feminist Theology

We can actually see that, more often than not, there is actually a very positive presentation of women in the Bible. Some of it does require some spin. For example, in the Genesis creation account, woman is created last and, thus, is the pinnacle of creation. (As the joke goes, why did God create man first? Practice![13]) But other passages and verses require no spin.

In Genesis 21:12, right after Abraham expels Hagar and Ishmael from his camp for something inappropriate happening with Isaac (see previous chapter), God tries to make Abraham feel good about this decision. He tells Abraham, "Do not be distressed because of the boy and because of your slave woman; *whatever Sarah says to you, do as she tells you ...* [emphasis my own]." Sarah is upset and concerned about the possibility of Ishmael getting a share of the inheritance due Isaac. (Interestingly, whenever God refers to Ishmael, he calls him a *na'ar* in Hebrew, which means "lad," whereas Abraham calls him *yeled*, meaning "child," denoting a biological link between them.) So, in a way, God is siding with Sarah and using her anger toward Ishmael and Hagar to help ensure his later test of Abraham would be carried out.[14]

Later, in Genesis 27, we see Isaac's children, Jacob and Esau, preparing for Isaac's death. Jacob has been identified as Rebekah's (Isaac's wife's) favorite of the two. When she hears Isaac tell Esau to get some game for him to eat, she knows Isaac is preparing to give Esau the blessing for his inheritance once he dies. When Esau goes to get the game, Rebekah dresses Jacob in furs, to resemble Esau's hairy body, and puts fragrances on him that resemble Esau's scent to fool Isaac. It works, and Rebekah secures Jacob's position as the future patriarch of the Israelites. This decision, never dictated by God, is approved by him only *after* the fact[15]—significantly, this demonstrates that God will approve of a decision made by a woman, even if he has not directed the decision.

In the following book of the Pentateuch, Exodus 1:15–22, we find a story that many are familiar with. It is the legend of the infancy of Moses, born to an Israelite while imprisoned in Egypt. According to this story, the Pharaoh, never mentioned by name, commands the death of all the male children of the Israelites. Moses' mother fears for her child and puts him in a papyrus basket and places him in the river, only to have him found by the daughter of the Pharaoh, who takes pity on him. He not only lives, but is also raised by his own mother as a wet nurse.

In Exodus 4:25, Moses is saved a third time by a woman—his wife, Zipphorah—when God attempts to kill him. In response, Zipphorah takes a flint, quickly circumcises their son, and holds the bloody foreskin to Moses' "feet," leading God to stop the fight. If you recall our earlier discussion on euphemisms, this implies that Zipphorah held the bloody foreskin to Moses' penis. When God sees the foreskin, he proclaims, "Truly you are a bridegroom of blood to me!" The word "bridegroom" in Hebrew is *hatan*, which means both "protected" and "circumcised." Whether Zipphorah wanted to make a connection to God's covenant with Abraham, or a link between marriage and circumcision, as is seen in Genesis 34:14–24, that is not entirely clear. What is clear is that Zipphorah is shown to be a strong female character, taking on a role predominantly carried out by men, as the circumcisers in Midianite and Israelite culture were expected to be (Genesis 17:23–27, Joshua 5:2–7, and in 1, 2, and 4 Maccabees). Not only does Zipphorah take on this strong, stereotypically "male" role by carrying out the circumcision, she also protects Moses during a battle with God.[16]

Women in the Bible are not only protectors but also merciless soldiers. Looking at the Book of Judges 5:19–23, Yael gives patronage to a soldier named Sisera who belittles her, referring to her in the masculine. When he falls asleep, she kills him. And, instead of facing negative repercussions, she is praised for this action; the author says it is according to divine will that she has executed him. "Most blessed of women be Yael . . . she struck Sisera a blow, she crushed his head, she shattered and pierced his temple." This story reverses the gender roles of men and women in battle. Instead of the male soldier penetrating the woman, Yael penetrates Sisera with her weapon. This story mirrors an old Canaanite tale, the Aqhat Epic, where a soldier named Aqhat angers the goddess Anat. While Aqhat is alone in his tent, Anat's servant, Yotpan, takes the form of a vulture, swoops down, and kills Aqhat by hitting him in the head.[17]

Similarly, in the Book of Judith, chapters 8–13, Judith has such beauty that, during the siege of Bethulia by the Assyrians, she is able to march through the city untouched and walk right up to the Assyrian general, Holofernes. He invites her to a banquet and, while he is passed out drunk, she "took hold of the hair of his head, and said, 'Give me strength today, O Lord God of Israel!' Then she struck his neck twice with all her might, and cut off his head." This story, if we read between the lines, offers nothing but a positive message—not only for women, but also for Israel. For starters, "Judith" is the feminine form of "Judean" or "Judas," which translates into the familiar "Jew" or "Jewish" title the people of Israel later take on. Her name also echoes that of the leader of the Maccabean revolt, Judas Maccabeus, furthering the idea of a strong, Jewish figure saving the people of Israel. The beheading also echoes the familiar battle between King David and Goliath in 1 Samuel 17:46. Additionally, Judith prays to Yahweh, the God of Israel, before taking action.[18][19] The author wrote this story with the intention of having a strong message for the people of Israel, regardless of the gender of the protagonist.

In the fifth chapter of the Book of Judges, there is a section known as the "Song of Deborah," a poem noted as being the earliest dated piece in the Hebrew Bible. Due to the very basic, archaic language used in the poem, and the battle that it details against the Canaanites, most scholars date this poem to the late twelfth century.[20] The poem reads, "You arose, Mother of Israel." Significantly, in the poem, Deborah is not listed as the "daughter of" or "wife of" or "sister of" anyone. She is only labeled, in Hebrew, as *'em beyisra'el*. That is, "Deborah, Mother of/in Israel." Has it sunk in yet? She is not defined as being the spouse or relative of any man, but as a woman who is the mother of the Israelite people. This clearly implies that, due to her title and the dating of the poem, Deborah was the first leader of the Israelite people—not David, nor Saul, but

Deborah. Further, she is the only military leader in Judges to be called a prophet.[21]

New Testament

Of course, it is not just in the Hebrew Bible that we find strong women in prominent positions. In the Book of Acts 16:11–15, we find women engaged in scriptural interpretation with Paul. In this particular section, the congregation has met at a *proseuches*, or house of prayer. As described in Acts, the individuals who attended the services, read, and prayed at the assembly were primarily women. In this story, we also see important ideas about women and the prominent roles they hold within the early church community, and even within synagogues.

Consider, for example, Lydia, a financially independent businesswoman identified in Acts 16:15 as the ruler of her household, which was baptized *with* her.[22] This fact demonstrates her authority, as dependents followed the head of the household in religious matters. We see evidence of this in Acts 18:18, where Crispus is the leader of his synagogue and his followers are all baptized with him. We also see it in 1 Corinthians 1:16, with the household of Stephanas.[23] More important perhaps to Lydia's story is her willingness to supervise the congregation within her own home, making her a patron of the faith.[24] We also see patrons like Joanna, the infamous Mary Magdalene, and Susanna, among "many others" implied to be women in Luke 8:1–3, who "provided for them out of their resources."[25]

In Acts 2:17–18, women act as oracles when they respond to the spirit of God , ". . . and your sons and daughters shall prophesy . . . Even upon my slaves, both men and women, in those days I will pour out my Spirit; and they shall prophesy." At 21:8–9, we meet Philip, an evangelist from Caesarea who has four unmarried daughters "who had the gift of prophecy." These four daughters later became important individuals for the church traditions surrounding Hierapolis and Ephesus, further demonstrating the importance of women within the early Church.[26]

Paul of Tarsus, perhaps more than anyone else in the New Testament, provides the strongest evidence for prominent female figures in the early Church. In his letter to the Romans, Paul writes of "Phoebe, a deacon [or minister] of the church at Cenchreae . . . for she has been a benefactor of many and of myself as well." In the same letter, Paul also mentions,

> *Prisca and Aquila, who work with me in Christ Jesus . . . Mary who has worked very hard among you . . . Junia, my relatives who were in prison with me; they are prominent among the apostles, and they were in Christ before I was . . . Greet those workers in The Lord, Tryphaena and Tryphosa. Greet the beloved Persis, who has worked hard in the Lord . . . and greet [Rufus'] mother—a mother to me also.*

Paul mentions other women in this chapter of Romans. Of the twenty-eight prominent figures referenced within just this church, ten of them are women. And one of them, Junia, is listed as "foremost among the apostles." This was enough for early church father John Chrysostom to invoke imagery of Junia in his sermon on women in the Church of Constantinople.[27] Other women who held strong leadership positions included Apphia, who presided over the church in Colossae, as seen in Philemon 1:2, and Nymphia in Laodicea in Colossians 4:15.

Say what you will about the Bible's rules and laws regarding women, it cannot be denied that the Bible tells the story of many remarkable women and notable leaders, going as far back as the beginning of the Israelite tribe in the twelfth century BCE. Women were patrons of the church and rulers of households. They were leaders in places of worship, and they were leaders of an entire group of people. What do sources outside of the biblical texts tell us about a woman's place in ancient Near Eastern society?

Outside of the Bible

Much like the Bible, other sources from antiquity view women in inconsistent and often contradictory ways. In Greek society, for example, notable figures like Plato, a philosopher from the fifth century BCE, wrote of the equality of men and women. Plato, as can be seen in his works *States* and *Laws*, writes more of gender equality than any other writer of his time, in complete contrast to his student Aristotle. Xenophon, another writer and historian from the same era, writes in *Oeconomicus* of the significant role of women in Greek society, their contributions, and their role in *oikos*, or families. This is not to say that, despite their advocacy for equality of women, these men, among many others, did not demean women. They certainly did. Xenophon, for example, notes that a woman's primary virtue is obedience. During this era, Greek society felt that women were a much weaker sex, that they enjoyed intercourse more than men, and that, by correlation, they were more prone to adultery. It was also thought that women could not share true, intimate, spiritual love with men. This was something only men could do with other men, hence the practice of pederasty, or homosexual relations between an adult male and pubescent or adolescent male.[28] But we will cover that more in a later chapter.

Women did hold strong spiritual positions during this era as well. For example, Alexander the Great, in the fourth century BCE, had a woman from Syria who provided oracles for him. Gaius Marius, a consul of the Roman Republic in the second century BCE, had a religious adviser who was a woman, and she provided oracles to his wife prior to becoming his adviser. And Plutarch, a Greek historian, wrote about female prophets who provided oracles that ended up saving the life of Cicero, a Roman philosopher.[29]

In the second century BCE, a cavalry officer in Ptolemais named Dryton had a wife, his second, named Apollonia. Upon the death of Dryton, Apollonia became the sole head of the household and inherited four slaves, a vineyard, a wagon, a dovecote, an oil press, and a grain mill. With such wealth, she would have been an independent woman and of similar status to Joanna in Luke or Lydia in Acts. Female landowners paid taxes, had legal liabilities, administered their own properties, and even oversaw small cottage industries like weaving, spinning, beer brewing, and even garland making for festivals.

The gnostic Secret Book of John, dated to the second century CE, has a female figure, Pronoia, who was a household leader who protected her dependents, collected payments due to her, and was a guardian of the resources provided to her and her business.[30] This example further demonstrates the cultural expectations for and roles of well-to-do women in ancient Greek and Roman society.

Going into the era of the early Church, we see a Christian movement associated with femininity and run by women. In the second century CE, Celsus, a Greek philosopher, attempted to discredit Christianity by labeling it as a women's movement.[31] Male patrons and leaders may have composed the public face of the early Church, but women ruled the house (or they at least shared responsibilities equally with the men). During the first two centuries of Christianity, the religion was practiced in the privacy of people's homes and out of the public sphere, which explains why it was affiliated with women, as Celsus suggests.[32]

What should be noted is that, in these societies, those who exercised patronage or had the means to do so would be put into positions of leadership in religious movements. As an example, in the late fourth or early fifth century CE, a woman named Myndos financed a decorated marble post for a synagogue, an inscription on which stated she was a "ruler of the synagogue." Similarly, a man in the third century CE, Klaudios Tiberius Polycharmos, donated part of his house to be used as a synagogue, and he was honored with the title "father of the synagogue." Leaders such as Myndos and Polycharmos, whether male or female, would collect taxes and mediate civil disputes between synagogue members.[33]

Other examples of female patronage from this era include, in Smyrna, "Rufina . . . head of the synagogue"; in Crete, "Sophia of Gortyn, elder and head of the synagogue of Kiasmos"; and, in Egypt, "Artemidoras . . . her mother Paniskianes being an elder." In addition, an epitaph for a woman who lived in the late fourth or early fifth century CE in Sicily reads, "Here lies Kale the elder."[34]

In addition to serving as patrons, women also served as spiritual leaders, such as Priscilla and Maximilla, two female prophets who worked with Phrygia Montanus.[35] Lucilla, who founded the African Church in the fourth century CE, earned patronage by providing financing to bishops in the Church, including Augustine, and enjoyed a higher social status than the clergy of the Carthaginian church.[36]

A very strong case for the leadership and independence of women in the era of Jesus is seen with Livia, the wife of the Roman emperor during Jesus' early life, Caesar Augustus. Among other things, Livia worked to secure Roman citizenship for clients from Gaul of low social ranking, provided patronage to the lower social classes during disasters, and gave dowries to daughters of families with little to offer in marriage, thus receiving their loyalty in return. These dowries provided financial security for women, as dowries could be returned in divorce and were essential for contracting a good marriage.[37]

Livia also convinced Augustus to show leniency when his political enemies were captured, thus winning their loyalty in future affairs. Seneca, a philosopher from the first century CE, wrote that Augustus thanked Livia for her counsel, stating he was "happy to have found a superior." And, because of her intelligence and good advice, Augustus gave Livia the right to manage her legal affairs without the presence of a male. Dio Cassius, a second-century historian, wrote that Livia acted as if she were the sole ruler of the empire, but he did note she was never known to have entered the public realm where men ruled. Upon her death, the cult of Augustus gave Livia the title of "priestess," and the senate decreed that an arch be erected in her honor, that she should be given the title of "mother" of the country, and that she should be granted divine honors. However, her son, the emperor Tiberius, being the chauvinist he was, clinged to societal expectations and stereotypes of women being subservient to men and denied her the right to be called parent of the country.[38]

So What Happened?

In the third century CE, the Mishnah, which is the writings of the oral tradition known as the Oral Torah, was composed. In this writing, a tractate labeled "Sotah," or "On the Suspect of Adulteress," addressed whether women should study the Torah. This tractate argues that women are overly sexual and likely to commit adultery. It is because of this, as well as ideals held by Greek and other surrounding cultures, that the Mishnah argues a husband should ensure that his wife does not study the Hebrew Bible.[39] Likewise, Rabbi Eliezer ben Hurcanus, a well-known Jewish religious figure from the first and second century CE, wrote, in the same document, "If a man gives his daughter knowledge of the law, it is as though he taught her lechery" (Mishnah Sotah 3:4).

Epiphanius, a bishop of Salamis on Cyprus in the fourth century, denounced female prophets because he called them "deceived and deranged," referring to one as "that deranged woman."[40] He felt that female prophets were contradictory to the Greco-Roman views of gender roles in society, so women who prophesied were misled and wrong.[41] Philo wrote in the first century that the marketplace, council halls, courts, assemblies of large crowds, and, really, any open place in public are meant for men. "But females appropriately keep the home and remain inside."[42] In this same writing, he argued that there is a greater state, which he elaborates is the city, and a lesser state, which is the household, and that the gender roles for the two states are male for the city and female for the house. In other words, public space is a male realm, and private space is a female one.[43]

Such a view was by no means unique. Tertullian wrote, "It is not permitted for a woman to speak in church ... not to baptize ... or offer ... claim for herself any manly function, least of all public office."[44] He believed not only that it was wrong for women to participate in public events as men do, but also that doing so made them act as men.[45] Similarly, John Chrysostom, despite having had his education financed by a woman, drew from the gender roles of his era in his polemics against the female Montanist prophets in the fourth century.

Aside from the issue of a woman being considered "damaged goods" if she slept with a man who wasn't her husband, either before or during marriage, the question of the paternity of children also contributed to men imposing constraints on the sexuality of women. Having a woman who was known to be a virgin at marriage and who lived under controlled conditions meant that any children produced would be the children of the husband. Thus, chastity was a virtue for women. Even writings like the Neopythagorean "Treatise on Chastity" advocated against private religious services due to the encouragement of "drunkenness and ecstasy." This virtue, in turn, was celebrated, explaining why we find things like the epitaph of Lady Pantheia, which stated that she had *sophrosyne*, or self-control. We also find writings honoring Lalla, a public priestess who was honored as being chaste and adherent to her husband. Even Livia, Augustus' wife, was praised for her chastity. At one point she even had nude male athletes arrested, eventually pardoning them, saying, "to chaste women, such men are no whit different than statues."[46]

Women are certainly expected to be silent and controlled by men, as seen both in 1 Timothy 2:11–12 and the writings of Plutarch: "control ought to be exercised by the man over the woman, not as the owner has control over a piece of property, but, as the soul controls the body, by entering into her feelings and being knit to her through goodwill."[47] In his book, *The Origin of Greek Thought*, Jean-Pierre Vernant writes, "Speech became the political tool par excellence, the key to all authority in the state, the means of commanding and dominating others."[48] With this in mind, we can make better sense of ancient epitaphs that praise women for their silence, such as, "She spoke little and was never rebuked," in reference to Allia Potestas, and the Aristotelian dictum that "silence is a woman's glory."[49] Tertullian wrote in *On Baptism*, "It is not permitted for a woman to speak in church, but neither is it permitted for her to teach, nor to baptize." A third-century church document, the *Didascalia,* states that women who exercise the right to minister are not demonstrating appropriate female behavior—namely, being passive and shy and showing restraint in the public domain.[50]

Do not think, for a minute, that this is where it ends. Tertullian, aside from insisting women needed to be silent and submissive to men, also felt it was not okay for women to wear too much makeup, as makeup presented a "false face" with which they would not be able to maintain their chastity. Livy wrote, in his *History of Rome*, that there was a vote on whether women had a right to wear jewelry, but women, at that time, were not allowed to vote! Augustine, in the fifth century, said that women were nothing but sexual beings and that, unlike women, men were made in God's image.[51] These arguments, among others made by the Church and church fathers, put all the responsibility of sexual immorality carried out by men on the shoulders of women. In other words, men could not be held accountable for their sexual urges—it was always the woman's fault.

In the Middle Ages, Heinrich Kramer, a German Catholic clergyman, argued in the *Malleus Maleficarum* (Witches' Hammer) that the title of "female" comes from *fe*, meaning "faith," and *minus*, meaning "less." So, to be female means to be "faithless." This gave justification to things like the Inquisition under Pope Innocent VIII in 1484, when more than one million women were burned at the stake for being witches and participating in sexual activities with the devil.[52]

However one wants to look at the information here, what cannot be denied is that religion has had a huge influence in how the treatment of women was shaped—whether in constraining their use of makeup and jewelry, their opportunities to talk, their freedom to choose their sexual partners, or even their opportunity to have sex at all. Religion made every effort to discourage them from acting, speaking, and, to a certain degree, even thinking without consent from a man.

Coming to the Americas

Prior to the "discovery" of the Americas, many of the native tribes there, like the Iroquois, were based on a matriarchal and matrilineal structure. Unlike in European and Near Eastern/ Middle Eastern societies, a man was inducted into a woman's family upon marriage. If a woman desired divorce, she could just place her husband's belongings outside of their dwelling, and it was done. Women also named the men who would represent their clan at their village tribal council, as well as the chiefs who made up the ruling council for the Five Nation Confederacy of Iroquois. Women attended clan meetings, removed men if they did not represent the women's needs in said meetings, tended crops, took over village affairs when men hunted and fished, and had control in military matters.[53]

This all changed with the arrival of Columbus, or more specifically, the Puritans, who believed Christianity needed to be imposed on the native populations. As justification, they cited biblical passages like Psalm 2:8, "Ask of me, and I shall give thee, the heathen for thine inheritance, and the uttermost parts of the earth for thy possession," and Romans 13:2, "Whosoever therefore resisteth the power, resisteth the ordinance of God: and they that resist shall receive to themselves damnation." The Puritans even invoked the wrath of God when they sacked villages. In *History of the Plymouth Plantation*, William Bradford writes of an attack on the Pequot tribe, "Those that scaped the fire were slaine with the sword . . . It was conceived they thus destroyed about 400 at this time . . . and [the Puritans] gave the prayers thereof to God, who had wrought so wonderfully for them, thus to inclose their enemise in their hands, and give them so speedy a victory over so proud and insulting an enimie." A puritan theologian, Dr. Cotton Mather, later wrote, "It was supposed that no less than 600 Pequot souls were brought down to hell that day."[54]

My purpose in writing the above is not to establish the reasons for the colonization, or the attacks on the native tribes of the Americas, but to establish what societies in the Americas looked like before the introduction of Christianity—before the forced implementation of a patriarchal culture.

In the early 1800s, Elizabeth Cady Stanton, daughter of Daniel Cady, a lawyer for the U.S. Congress and a New York Supreme Court justice, discovered some rather startling information about the so-called doctrine of coverture, which, in essence, made a woman nonexistent once she married. This doctrine stemmed from the Book of Genesis 3:16: "To the woman he said, 'I will greatly increase your pangs in childbearing; in pain you shall bring forth children, yet your desire shall be for your husband, and he shall rule over you.'" This doctrine said that when a woman married and took her husband's last name, the woman lost her identity and her legal existence was suspended during the marriage. Any legal action, very much like in first-century Rome (recall the story of Livia, who was given the right to perform legal action without a male presence), had to be carried out by the husband or done in his name. Contracts, as an example, could not be entered without the husband's name on the document. Further, any property a woman brought into the marriage became legally owned by the husband, unless it was placed in a trust. Even then, the woman lost control of the property once entered into marriage, and she also could not accrue the husband's property because, very much like in antiquity, it would go instead to the first male heir. Even a will created prior to a marriage essentially dissolved after marriage, as the property entrusted to her would no longer be considered, legally, her own.[55]

Stanton, being a woman and seeing the injustice in such a doctrine, was outraged by this. Taking the information her father had taught her, she went to work fighting against the doctrine of coverture, and fighting for women's rights. Her biggest fight, however, was not necessarily the law itself, but the idea people had that she was fighting against the word of God. "The masses believe the Bible is directly from God; that it decrees the inequality of the sexes, and that settles the question," wrote William Lloyd Garrison. Edward Mansfield, in a treatise titled, "The Legal Rights, Liabilities, and Duties of Women," wrote that marriage is "an institution of God . . . begun in the Garden of Eden . . . men must govern their families, and women submit to their lawful requisitions." And, very much like a continuation of the ancient view of the public role of women, women were also not permitted to take part in public life, due to Eve's "sin" in the Garden of Eden. Even in a couple's personal life, the husband had an unfair advantage. In cases of adultery, a man's infidelity would not abrogate the marital contract as a woman's would. Chancellor James Kent wrote that unfaithfulness by a husband "is not evidence of such entire depravity, not equally injurious in its effects upon the morals, good order, and happiness of domestic life," as the unfaithfulness of a wife. It would appear that women were pressured to be the agents of morality when it came to reproduction, but not competent enough to participate in society without their husbands by their side.[56]

This is not to say there were not movements to help women, but even they held the idea that Protestant Christianity was the moral, and correct, choice for all of the United States' citizens. In 1887, the U.S. Congress enacted the Edmunds-Tucker Act. This act was an attempt to restrict the practices of the Church of Jesus Christ of Latter-day Saints, specifically polygamy, with a fine of 500 to 800 dollars and imprisonment up to five years. It also enabled the federal government to confiscate property owned by the Mormon Church.[57]

Legal moves like these eventually gave rise to a movement that begin in the 1970s called Dominionism. This movement, derived from Genesis 1:26–31, where God calls for humanity to have dominion over all the life on the planet, sought to politicize the Christian faith. Movement followers believed that the Decalogue should serve as the basis for the legal system, that education should be based on creationism and Christian values, and that labor unions, civil-rights laws, and public schools should be abolished. For our purposes, however, the salient point is that Dominionism dictated that women should be removed from the work force in order to stay at home and care for the homestead and raise their families.[58] On of the leading thinkers behind this movement, R. J. Rushdoony, even argued that women should receive the death penalty for being "unchaste before marriage."[59]

The desire to impose restrictions and punishments on women has gained currency and support among some politicians and voters. In 2004, for example, a Republican senator from South Carolina, Jim DeMint, pushed to restrict single mothers and gay men from teaching in schools.[60] So-called red states, those that are predominantly Republican with a large evangelical Christian following, may have higher rates of illegitimate and teen births than less religious states, but that has not stopped them from slashing funding to public education and cutting significantly assistance to women through the Women, Infants, and Children Supplemental Nutrition Program (WICSNP).[61]

While the people who hold a Dominionist worldview believe women who do not submit to men are going against the word of God, men within this movement seem to function under a veil of hypermasculinity—perhaps as a means of compensation for their own submission to an all-powerful male deity. Jerry Falwell, during a sermon at the Temple Baptist Church in 1986, said he gave his wife what she wanted because he chose to, not because he had to. He also claimed to never think about divorce, but he did think about murdering her a few times.[62] Charming. Christian conservative leader James Dobson has stated that there are "countless physiological and emotional differences between the sexes." For example, he feels women need love, where men do not. According to him, "man is master, woman must obey"—or, at least, that is the message he draws from the Book of Genesis. Joseph Nicolosi, author, with his wife Linda Ames Nicolosi, of *A Parent's Guide to Preventing Homosexuality*, argues that to prevent boys from being or becoming gay in the first place, "boys need strong male figures who don't submit to women."

Other women are actively involved in the movement. Consider Beverly LaHaye, the wife of *Left Behind* author Tim LaHaye, who founded an antifeminist group known as Concerned Women of America. She has stated that the

United States is ruled by "evil" organizations like the National Organization for Women, Planned Parenthood, and even the American Civil Liberties Union and National Association for the Advancement of Colored People.[63] You have to wonder, given all that we have discussed, what sort of influence and hold this movement has when a woman feels she needs to *start* an organization to counter those who fight for the very demographic she is a part of.

Conclusion

It is hard to completely deny the misogyny within the Bible; its authors wrote it during a different time, during different socioeconomic circumstances, with hardly any concept of the world around them. Laws and rules were set up to ensure that families stayed together and that property was proerly protected—or, at the very least, to ensure that paternity was not in question and that a stable population was maintained. The question truly becomes, then, was the Bible written with the intention of being a timeless work whose rules could be followed across not only generations but also centuries and even millennia? Well . . .

The problems women in the United States face today, such as a gender-based pay gap, a lack of access to important resources, a denial of their bodily autonomy, and physical violence, may all have roots in the ancient world, but today's technological landscape has given them new life. For example, consider the situation of *Hunger Games* star Jennifer Lawrence, whose iCloud account was reportedly hacked in 2014, leading to privately taken nude photos of her being posted online without her permission or consent. She likely never intended for more than one individual to see those photos, and clearly never intended for them to be made public. Regardless of her reason for taking the photos, people should not belittle, insult, humiliate, or slut shame someone for what they choose to do with their body.

So what is my point? My point is we live in a patriarchal society in which, thanks in large part to the influence of misogynist church fathers multiple centuries ago, we do not give women an equal opportunity. Thank people like Tertullian, who said wearing too much makeup did not permit women to maintain chastity, and Augustine, who felt that women were nothing but sexual beings.[64] While these actions and words—among countless others over the centuries—may in themselves have made only little ripples in the fabric of society, the collective wave of injustice, misogyny, prejudice, shaming, and harm to women created by them is undeniable.

Notes

1. *National Committee on Pay Equity*, http://www.pay-equity.org (accessed December 26, 2014).

2. See Philip Cohen, "'Women Own 1% of World Property,'" *Atlantic*, March 8, 2013, http://www.theatlantic.com/sexes/archive/2013/03/women-own-1-of-world-property-a-feminist-myth-that-wont-die/273840/.

3. RAINN, "Who Are the Victims?" https://rainn.org/get-information/statistics/sexual-assault-victims.

4. Pagels, *Serpent*, 13.

5. Carr, *Annotated*, 12–13.

6. Carr, *Annotated*, 14–15.

7. Friedman and Dolansky, *The Bible Now*, 79, 81.

8. Friedman and Dolansky, *The Bible Now*, 77–78.

9. John Barclay, "1 Corinthians," in *The Oxford Bible Commentary* (New York: Oxford University Press, 2001), 1125.

10. Ehrman, *The New Testament*, 292–93.

11. Mitchell, *Annotated*, 2087.

12. Ehrman, *The New Testament*, 443–444.

13. Friedman and Dolansky, *The Bible Now*, 77.

14. Hamilton, *Genesis: Chapters 18–50*, 81.

15. Friedman and Dolansky, *The Bible Now*, 87–88.

16. Carol Meyers, "Exodus," in *The New Oxford Annotated Bible* (New York: Oxford University Press, 2010), 88.

17. Tikva Frymer-Kensky, *Reading the Women of the Bible* (New York: Schocken Books, 2002), 56.

18. Frymer-Kensky, *Reading*, 55.

19. Lawrence M. Wills, "Judith," in *The New Oxford Annotated Bible* (New York: Oxford University Press, 2010), 1405.

20. Carol L. Meyers, "Deborah," in *The Oxford Guide to the Bible* (New York: Oxford University Press, 1993), 161.

21. Friedman and Dolansky, *The Bible Now*, 68–69.

22. Karen Jo Torjesen, *When Women Were Priests* (New York: Harper Collins Press, 1993), 14–15.

23. Christopher R. Matthews, "Acts," in *The New Oxford Annotated Bible* (New York: Oxford University Press, 2010), 1950.

24. Torjesen, *Priests*, 33.

25. Marion L. Soards, "Luke," in *The New Oxford Annotated Bible* (New York: Oxford University Press, 2010), 1844.

26. Matthews, *Annotated*, 1959.

27. Torjesen, *Priests*, 33.

28. Nissinen, *Homoeroticism*, 64.

29. Torjesen, *Priests*, 28.

30. Torjesen, *Priests*, 56–57.

31. Torjesen, *Priests*, 76.

32. Origen, *Contra Celsus*, ch. 55, translated in vol. 4 of *The Ante-Nicene Fathers*, 1867–1872, http://www.bluffton. edu/˜humanities/1/celsus.htm (accessed September 1, 2014).

33. Torjesen, *Priests*, 18.

34. Torjesen, *Priests*, 19, 20, 25.

35. According to Eusebius in *Historia Ecclesia* (2.25; 3.31; 4.20).

36. Torjesen, *Priests*, 91.

37. Torjesen, *Priests*.

38. Torjesen, *Priests*, 96–97, 102, 104.

39. Tirzah Meacham (leBeit Yoreh), "Legal-Religious Status of theSuspected Adulteress (Sotah)," in *Jewish Women's Archive: A Comprehensive Historical Encyclopedia*, March 1, 2009, http://tinyurl. com/kwltkhr (accessed December 27, 2014).

40. Karen Thorjesen, "Wisdom, Christology, and Women Prophets," in *Jesus Then and Now: Images of Jesus in History and Christology*, ed. Marvin Meyer and Charles Hughes (London: Bloomsbury Publishing, 2001), 186.

41. Torjesen, *Priests*, 44.

42. In *Special Laws* 3.169.

43. Kenneth Schenck, *A Brief Guide to Philo* (Louisville: Westminster John Knox Press, 2005), 68.

44. In *On the Veilings of Virgins* 9:1.

45. Matthew Kuefler, *The Manly Eunuch: Masculinity, Gender Ambiguity, and Christian Ideology in Late Antiquity* (Chicago:

University of Chicago Press, 2001), 228.

46. Torjesen, *Priests*, 119, 123, 144.

47. Plutarch, *Conjugalia Praecepta*, "Advice to Bride and Groom," section 33 (Chicago: University of Chicago Press, 1928), http://tinyurl.com/6g9u49.

48. Jean-Pierre Vernant, *The Origins of Greek Thought* (Ithica: Cornell University Press, 1984), 49.

49. In *Politics* 1:13.

50. As cited in Torjesen, *Priests*, 119, 144.

51. Torjesen, *Priests,* 158, 221.

52. As cited in Torjesen, *Priests*, 229.

53. Howard Zinn, *A People's History of the United States* (New York: Harper Perennial Press, 2005), 20.

54. Zinn, *History*, 14–15.

55. Sehat, *Myth*, 98.

56. Sehat, *Myth*, 101–4.

57. Lola Van Wagenen, *Sister-Wives and Suffragists: Polygamy and the Politics of Woman Suffrage, 1870–1896* (New York: New York University Press, 2001).

58. Hedges, *Fascists*, 10–12.

59. R. J. Rushdoony, "Institutes of Biblical Law," *Christ Rules*, 1973, http://www.christrules.com/biblical-law (accessed September 1, 2014).

60. Amanda Terkel, "Sen. Jim DeMint: Gays and Unmarried, Pregnant Women Should Not Teach Public School," *Huffington Post*, October 2, 2010, http://tinyurl.com/38g29rx (accessed July 12, 2014).

61. Hedges, *Fascists*, 46.

62. Hedges, *Fascists*, 88.

63. Hedges, *Fascists*, 85, 101–102, 188.

64. Willemien Otten, "Augustine on Marriage, Monasticism, and the Community of the Church," *Theological Studies* 59, no.3 (1998): 386, http://tinyurl.com/qdpzh4v.

3

Abortion

On June 27, 2014, the U.S. Supreme Court struck down a buffer-zone law around abortion clinics, siding with those who argued that it was unconstitutional to have buffer zones around clinics because they kept protestors from offering "counseling" and "assistance" to those who sought abortions.[1] As the Huffington Post pointed out, the Supreme Court demonstrated pure hypocrisy with this ruling, as it has its own buffer zone to keep out protestors.[2] Though little consolation, states may continue to enforce laws prohibiting protestors from blocking the entrance to clinics, which allows women to at least enter clinics without someone standing in their way, because the justices let stand a decision from *Hill v. Colorado* that prohibited protesting within eight feet of someone entering a clinic or healthcare facility. Even so, Catholic Supreme Court justice Anthony Scalia believed the Hill ruling should be overturned.[3]

All said, abortion is certainly a touchy subject. Allowing clinic-adjacent opportunities for those who support anti-abortion ideologies to espouse their opinions makes things even harder for those individuals who have already made the conscious, and often difficult, decision to abort a pregnancy. "I think it's clear that when you have a number of patients or volunteers saying they feel intimidated or harassed, it's a problem, and it's a bigger problem than we can solve at the facility," said Jill Krowinski, who is the vice president of education and Vermont community affairs for Planned Parenthood of Northern New England. She said this several months after the overturning of the buffer-zone law, which had forbidden protestors from being on the same side of the street as the clinic, now using the title "sidewalk counselors."[4]

These phony "sidewalk counselors," who also advocate for various therapies and counseling online, cause more problems than they create. The anti-abortion Web site HopeAfterAbortion.org, for example, promotes Project Rachel, "which helps mothers and fathers find forgiveness and healing"—something presumably needed because "abortion destroys more than an innocent child's life. It can shatter a woman's peace, happiness, sense of self-worth, her goals, and relationships." Such "counselors" make other rather startling claims—for example, that women who have an abortion are 81 percent more likely to have mental health issues than women who have not. Project Rachel also claims that those who have an abortion have a 34 percent higher rate of anxiety, 37 percent higher rate of depression, 110 percent higher rate of alcohol abuse, 230 percent higher rate of marijuana use, and a 155 percent higher rate of suicidal behavior. Such "counselors" also allege that abortion contributes greatly to the risk of PTSD, panic disorders, drug and alcohol dependency, and major depression.

While these and other such claims are made by anti-abortion proponents, what do legitimate scientific studies tell us about abortion and women's health? A July 2010 study from the University of California, San Francisco (UCSF) Medical Center titled "Mental Health Issues and Abortion" demonstrated that there is no significant difference between women who abort a pregnancy and women who choose to continue a pregnancy through to birth. And, very clearly, a woman's mental health post-abortion depends a lot on her mental health prior to the abortion. Ideas like "post-abortion syndrome," as is seen on anti-choice sites like CatholicNewsAgency.com, are entirely fictional.[5] The Huffington Post ran an article on this so-called syndrome whose title tells you everything you need to know about it: "Post Abortion-Syndrome: The Solution in Search of a Problem."[6] In fact, the UCSF study shows that the most common feeling women have post-abortion is not anxiety, suicidal thoughts, or depression, but relief. Any negative feelings afterward stem from pre-abortion mental health issues, preexisting conflicted views toward abortion, lack of social support, and (get ready for the big surprise) exposure to protestors outside of the clinic. Each of these factors, especially those that come with social stigma, increase the likelihood of negative emotions after the procedure is done.[7]

The UCSF study, in discussing the legitimate mental health–related side effects of abortion, states that papers which suggest "post-abortion syndrome" is a real thing are sloppy and show faulty methodology. The study demonstrates that the authors of such papers make inappropriate assumptions and comparisons and do not control the groups for prior mental health issues and depression. The authors also confuse causality and association. Perhaps most significantly, the results of "post-abortion syndrome" studies cannot be replicated. More troubling still, just as those who advocate for intelligent design create their own organizations and biased peer-review systems to attempt to give legitimacy to their opinions and beliefs,[8] so too do anti-choice proponents.[9]

Other studies similarly show the damage caused by anti-choice groups. For example, the American Psychological Association (APA) found that "women who come to internalize the stigma associated with abortion are likely to be particularly vulnerable to later psychological distress" and, thus, will create a self-fulfilling prophecy when they are told they "should" or "will" feel negative emotions after having abortion. As the APA study shows, there is no greater mental-health risk for a woman aborting a wanted pregnancy than there is for a woman who miscarried a wanted pregnancy.[10]

We also have incredibly "insightful" opinions from people like the late Pope John Paul II who said, in "the Gospel of Life no. 58," that abortion is "direct killing, by whatever means it is carried out, of a human being in the initial phase of his or her existence." This is a continuation of long-standing Catholic ideology, which holds that human life comes into being at the moment of conception—the moment the sperm fuses with the egg after intercourse. However, this does not take into account fetal viability, or the idea of whether a fetus can breathe without support from the mother's own body.

Studies have found that approximately 30 percent of fetuses born at 23 weeks survive, and that number increases with each ensuing week. At 24 weeks, there is a 50–60 percent chance of survival, 75 percent at 25 weeks, and 90 percent or more at 27–28 weeks. In the United States, a fetus is considered viable at the 24-week mark. The survival rate of fetuses that leave the womb prior to that point is extremely low, while those that do survive are very likely to have a handicap due to the complications of such a premature birth.[11]

What Does the Bible Say?

Nothing.[12] This is not an oversimplification. The Bible says absolutely nothing on the practice of abortion. And this is not a means of glossing over sections, ignoring particular passages, using hermeneutics to understand passages in a different light, or employing any other theological filter. The Bible says not a single thing on the practice of abortion, even though it was practiced in the ancient world. From where, then, do so-called biblical arguments against abortion come from?

The obvious place to start is in the Decalogue, which states, at Exodus 20:13, "You shall not murder." Note, the prohibition is against murdering and not killing. Specifically, the Hebrew word used in this commandment is *rsh*, meaning "murder," and not *mwt*, meaning "kill." These two words are often conflated, but there is a clear distinction between them. So, if we are to demonstrate that abortion is in direct opposition to this commandment, we first would need to show that abortion represents the *murder* of a child.

But what does it mean to *murder*? The legal definition of murder, as would be defined in a legal proceeding against an individual tried for such a crime, is "the killing of a human being . . . with intent, malice aforethought . . . and with no legal excuse or authority."[13]

The first part of this definition raises a number of important questions of its own—some philosophical, some rather black and white. Specifically, what does it mean to be a human being? This goes back to viability. We can argue that a fetus is a *potential* human being, but until it reaches a point in utero where it is capable of survival outside the mother's body, it is, from a legal standpoint, not considered a human being. Seeing that 90 percent of abortions take place during the first trimester, or the first twelve weeks, of pregnancy, then by extension the vast majority of abortions cannot be considered or defined as murder.

Looking at the second part of the definition of murder, can we say that a woman has an abortion with malice? That may be hard to determine in individual cases, but—based on the available evidence—there is generally a great sense of relief after the procedure, and maybe a sense of anxiety prior to the procedure. No reputable study suggests malice is ever part of the equation.

Abortion is of course legal in the United States and does not fit under the legal definition of murder. Indeed, the United States currently permits abortion to save a woman's life and to preserve her physical health, and for cases of rape or incest, for reasons related to fetal impairments, for economic or social reasons, and even, yes, for simple "on-request" reasons. The U.S. government even provides direct support for family planning.[14] Given this context, it is incorrect to argue that abortion is murder, or is in opposition to the Decalogue.

What other possible biblical cues against abortion might there be? Exodus 21:22–25 describes a law relating to miscarriage caused in a discrete circumstance. Specifically, if a pregnant woman is inadvertently hit in the stomach by a man having an altercation with her husband and has a miscarriage, the offender has to pay the husband what he, and "the judges," determine is owed to him. This law, however, does not infer a biblical objection to abortion, as this passage describes an action by a third party that unintentionally results in miscarriage. More so, the law does not clarify if the penalty is for harm to the woman or for the miscarriage, but it does offer a large clue toward the biblical view of fetal death. Indeed, the passage that follows reference to the death of the fetus states, "and there is no harm . . ." The implication is obvious: causing the death of a fetus was not considered a serious offense.[15]

Other ancient laws provide a bit of context. Paralleling the Exodus passage, the Code of Hammurapi has a similar law, where ten shekels of silver are paid for the fetus. Contrast that with the punishment if the woman dies in the altercation: the daughter of the offender is to be killed. A Hittite law, outlining similar circumstances, demands monetary compensation based on the father's input. A Middle Assyrian law holds that, if the wife miscarries, the offender has to give the victim a child from his own household. Even worse, should the father not have any sons, and the mother miscarries, the offender is executed.[16]

What is important to understand is that all of these laws related more to the protection of the wife—and to the protection of the father's familial line—than to the actual fetus being carried. Thus, to assume that Exodus provides a prohibition against abortion is a very large stretch.

A biblical passage that actually expresses a wish *for* abortion is Jeremiah 20:14–18. Here, Jeremiah bemoans, "Cursed be the day on which I was born! The day when my mother bore me, let it not be blessed . . . because he did not kill me in the womb; so my mother would have been my grave." Reflecting on our discussion about the Decalogue, Jeremiah uses the word *mwt,* or "kill"—and not *rsh,* or "murder."[17] Further, the dramatics of the passage suggest that life does not truly begin until birth, which stands in contrast to Jeremiah 1:5: "Before I formed you in the womb I knew you, and before you were born I consecrated you." While these passages suggest beliefs about when life begins, they relate to communication to and by one person: Jeremiah. Unlike other biblical passages that more explicitly relate to the moment life begins, such as in Genesis, as we will see, there is no context here that universalizes these passages to all of humanity.

For other instances related to the killing, or murder, of a fetus, we can look elsewhere in the Bible. In the Book of Job 3:16, Job says, "Oh why was I not buried like a stillborn child, like an infant that never sees the light?" The Hebrew word used for "stillborn" is *nepel,* which does not refer to a "killed" or "murdered" fetus. A similar example is at Ecclesiastes 4:1–3, which speaks of praises for "the dead, who have already died, more fortunate than the living, who are still alive; but better than both is the one who has not yet been, and has not seen the evil deeds that are done under the sun."

Perhaps more relevant to this discussion are the biblical passages specifically about when life begins. Looking at

Genesis 2:7, we read, "then the LORD God formed man from the dust of the ground, and breathed into his nostrils the breath of life; and the man became a living being." So, the first man becomes alive when he has "the breath of life" blown, or breathed, into his nostrils. Continuing at Genesis 6:17, God says to Noah, "I am going to bring a flood of waters on the earth, to destroy from under heaven all flesh in which is the breath of life, everything that is on earth shall die." Again, the *breath* of life. An interesting trend is starting. At Genesis 7:15, "They went into the ark with Noah, two and two of all flesh in which there was the breath of life." There is that breath of life again, but let us look at one more passage just to be certain this is really what gives life. Genesis 7:22 states, "everything on dry land in whose nostrils was the breath of life died."[18]

Now, just to be clear, what can we learn of the breath of life from these accounts? Well, according to Genesis, if we look at the creation story with Adam, or *adamah*, which is Hebrew for "dust" (*adam* is Hebrew for "man" or "humanity"), we see God's breath—the breath of life—animating the dust, making it a living being.[19] By extension, we can conclude that all, humanity, all the flesh of the earth, and everything on dry land needed "the breath of life" to become alive. Thus, if we take a literal reading of the Bible, abortion could not possibly equate to murder, or killing of any kind, as the potential for life has not yet *become* life.

Abortion Outside of the Bible

Abortion is actually an incredibly ancient practice. The earliest reference we have for abortion comes from the Ebers Papyrus of Egypt, which dates to 1550–1500 BCE, or roughly three centuries before our earliest evidence for the people of Israel. The Ebers Papyrus was a medical text that provided instructions on how to perform abortions.[20] Ancient abortion was typically nonsurgical. Practices included lifting heavy objects, paddling, fasting, and blood-letting.[21] Even the stoics, dating around the third century BCE, found abortion acceptable because they viewed the fetus as plant like while in the womb, and not as "alive" until the moment of birth.[22]

Prior to stoicism, in the mid fourth century BCE, Aristotle, the Greek philosopher and scientist, supported abortion as well. He did not view a fetus as being alive, or even having a soul, until a particular number of days had passed after conception: forty days if it were male, and ninety days if it were female.[24] To determine the sex of a fetus, the Greeks employed various practices. For example, they could allegedly determine the sex depending on which side of the body the fetus rested on while in utero—right for male, left for female.[23] Even before conception, men were known to tie one of their testicles, with the hope of increasing their chances for having a child of one sex or another.

After the final writings of the New Testament, the first Christian book of any kind to address abortion was *The Didache*, an early Jewish-Christian treatise that dates to the mid-second century CE.[25] While the actual Bible—both the New Testament and the Hebrew Bible—says nothing on abortion, *The Didache* very specifically says, "do not murder a child by abortion or kill a newborn infant." Other noncanonical texts not included among the books of the New Testament, like the second-century CE Epistle of Barnabas and the Apocalypse of Peter, denounce abortion, but they do not equate it to murder. The Apocalypse of Peter 8 speaks of women "who have caused their children to be born untimely and have corrupted the work of God who created them." In chapter 7, however, it speaks of a punishment for those who are murderers but makes no mention of abortion.[26] The Epistle of Barnabas 19:5, meanwhile, makes a clear distinction between aborting a fetus and killing a child, as the author refers to these acts as being independent of one another.[27] Regardless, because these texts are not part of canonized scripture, there existence provides no biblical basis for either supporting abortion or equating it to murder.

After these texts were written, Clement of Alexandria (150–215 CE), one of the early church fathers, taught some rather revolutionary practices in the still young Christian movement. Taking on a rather Pauline stream of belief, he taught that Jesus of Nazareth had come to change marital patterns so that men were superior to women, according to God's punishment of Eve in the Garden of Eden. More than that, he claimed that Jesus had completely dissolved any and all pagan sexual and marital practices, including homosexuality, infanticide, divorce, and abortion.[28]

John Chrysostom (347–407 CE), another church father, also wrote about abortion. In his *Homily 24 on Romans*, Chrysostom wrote that abortion was equivalent to murder—and that this murder begins with drunkenness, which leads to "whoredom" or, in other words, adultery.[29] Later still, Thomas Aquinas, a friar and theologian during the thirteenth century CE, wrote a piece called *Summa Theologica*. This piece was intended as an instructional guide on the teachings of the Church. Inside, Aquinas wrote of abortion—specifically, that abortion was permitted up until "the quickening." "The quickening" was similar to the stoics' idea of "ensoulment." According to Aquinas, the fetus did not possess a soul until forty days after conception, and therefore abortion was permitted so long as it happened prior to the quickening.[30]

Centuries before this, Augustine of Hippo (354–430 CE) wrote a number of times about abortion. In those cases when he advocated against abortion, he did so in reference to "pagan" sexual acts, including adultery.[31] In *Enchiridion* 23.86, he wrote, "Now, from the time that a man beings to live . . . ," without saying when that point is. Elsewhere in his writings, it is clear he also believed in ensoulment—that a fetus was not "alive" if it it had not yet obtained a soul, as seen in his commentary on the Septuagint version of Exodus 21:22–23.

These early church fathers clearly did not view abortion the way most conservative contemporary religious leaders do, with many even prescribing a permissible time frame to perform an abortion. In addition, these men viewed the practice as one associated with those who were not of the Christian faith. Thus, the practice of abortion was seen as an identifier for those who did not practice the faith, and any commands or prescriptions they may have given against abortion must be understood in this context.

With all this in mind, then, how did we get to the modern idea that a fetus is a living person and that abortion is murder, regardless of what stage of the pregnancy the woman is in? Well, we can thank John Calvin for this. In his commentary on Exodus, Calvin says, "the unborn . . . is already a human being."[32] Setting the stage for the belief the faithful have clung to for centuries since, Calvin's views on the matter may very well be the reason women who have had, want to have, or need to have an abortion face such stigma today.

So What Happened?

Aside from the aforementioned statements by church fathers and other theologians whose opinions the faithful cling to, a number of things happened that created strong opinions and outrage over abortion, especially in the United States. In 1973, the well-known *Roe v. Wade* case brought into effect a law that utilized a privacy doctrine, doing away with hospital "therapeutic abortion boards" charged with making determinations about whether a doctor could perform an abortion on a case-by-case basis. The U.S. Supreme Court ruled that the decision to have an abortion was a private, moral choice made by the woman and that the state had no business in her decision. Associate Justice Harry Blackmun, appointed by President Richard Nixon and author of the Court's opinion, made it so that states could enforce regulations only once the fetus was viable. The decision helped strengthen U.S. citizens' right to privacy and the notion that an individual alone, and not the state, is responsible for personal moral decisions.[33]

Conservatives, meanwhile, were absolutely furious over the decision and its outcome, with outraged Catholics, evangelicals, and fundamentalists banding together to continue their fight against a practice they equate with murder. They felt the outcome would produce anarchy, a society that would completely implode. In the wake of the ruling, presuppositionalist theologian Frank Schaeffer created a book and documentary series titled "How Should We Live?" And what a series it was! His series exploded in popularity when he covered the topic of abortion and discussed how "liberal radicals" sought the "abolition of truth and morality."[34] Mobilizing evangelicals in their fight against legal abortion, his words helped give rise to the politically active Christian Right.

Despite the Supreme Court decision, conservatives proved they were not all talk. In 1977, in *Maher v. Wade*, a six-to-three decision stated that states would not have to fund nontherapeutic abortions for women on welfare. Thankfully, Associate Justice William J. Brennan, in his dissenting opinion, argued states could not infringe on the rights of others, specifically minorities, by inhibiting the practice of abortion through legislature. It was shown that, because the *Roe v. Wade* decision was a private, personal decision, it could not be up to the state to decide what was therapeutic or not. That did not stop Henry Hyde, a Catholic Republican from Illinois, from placing an amendment in an unrelated bill in 1980 that would have prohibited federal funding for abortions, even if such a procedure was necessary for the mother's health. The bill that contained this amendment was struck down and overturned in district court, which stated that the bill was not just about a religious issue but "traditionalist values towards abortion."[35]

The fight continues on: George W. Bush, as Texas governor in 1999, said, if he was elected President, he would appoint only anti-abortion judges to the Supreme Court, a promise he fulfilled. Chief Justice John G. Roberts, nominated by President George W. Bush, upheld a federal law that had limited abortions and denied women the right to sue for discrimination based on sex.[36] In 2004, Tom Coburn, a Republican senator from Oklahoma, requested a ban on abortion and suggested the death penalty for doctors who performed the procedure, as did James Dobson, founder of Focus on the Family, an anti-abortion, fundamentalist Christian organization, who also stated that *Roe v. Wade* brought upon the United States the "biggest holocaust in world history." Bill McCarthy, founder of the men's rights group Promise Keepers, called abortion the "second civil war." Pat Robertson, the well-known evangelical and chairman of the Christian Broadcasting Network, blamed the terrorist attacks of September 11, 2001 on abortion.[37]

Conclusion

The stigma surrounding abortion is severely misplaced. What much of our society thinks it knows about abortion comes from a lack of education—even a complete miseducation on the subject. If a person decides that an abortion is ethically not something they would want when they are pregnant, then it is perfectly acceptable for them to forgo the abortion. However, for people to impose their own sense of morality onto others who face an already difficult decision—and to assume that, because their beliefs are right for them, they should be right for everyone—is a demonstrably poor and harmful action.

What we see is a group of people telling other people not to perform, consent to, or take part in abortions because the group members believe a piece of literature that is alleged to be divinely inspired says doing so is wrong. Assuming even for a moment the Bible was divinely inspired, there is no mention in its pages, not even to the slightest degree, of anything pertaining to abortion. The Christian Right has misattributed biblical laws that do not relate to abortion, assumed passages that refer to one individual to speak to all of humanity, and taken cues from later church fathers and religious leaders who spoke against abortion based on their own extremely limited knowledge of the human body and fetal development. Remember, this was a time when humanity thought that men, through intercourse, placed the baby inside the woman—and that she simply carried and grew the baby in her womb.

More than all of that, we see people shaming women for making a private, personal choice about their own bodies. Up until the time a fetus is truly viable, it is only a *potential* human life that is using another person's body to survive. If we outlaw abortions, then we will, in effect, be giving more freedom to the deceased, whose bodies we cannot use for organ donations or scientific research without their prior consent, than to living women. Just as we are under no obligation to provide plasma or bone marrow to help save the life of another individual, so too should women be free to decide whether they want a fetus developing inside of them. When we vilify abortion, then we vilify a woman's right to choose what she does with her body—a personal decision that should be made by the individual and no one else.

Notes

1. Amy Howe, "Court Strikes Down Abortion Clinic Buffer Zone in Plain English," SCOTUS Blog, June 27, 2014, http://scotusblog.com/2014/06/court-strikes-down-abortion-clinic-buffer-zone-in-plain-english.

2.   Amanda Terkel, "Supreme Court Rules Against Buffer Zones from Behind Its Own Buffer Zone," *Huffington Post*, June 26, 2014, m.huffpost.com/entry/5533389.

3.   Alana Semuels, "Abortion Buffer Zone Laws Begin Falling after Supreme Court Ruling," *Los Angeles Times*, July 7, 2014, www.latimes.com/nation/nationnow/la-na-nn-buffer-zone-laws-struck-down-20140707-story.html.

4.   Alicia Freese, "Burlington Seeks Alternative to Clinic Buffer Zone," *Seven Days*, September 10, 2014, www.sevendaysvt.com/vermont/burlington-seeks-alternative-to-clinic-buffer-zone/Content?oid=2435026.

5.   "Mental Health Issues and Abortion," Advancing New Studies in Reproductive Health, UCSF Medical Center, July 2010, http://www.ansirh.org/research/late-abortion/countering-misinformation/mental-health-abortion.php. For the anti-choice position on the matter, see "Post-Abortion Syndrome," Catholic News Agency, http://www.catholicnewsagency.com/resources/abortion/after-an-abortion/post-abortion-syndrome-pas/.

6.   Sarah Erdreich, "Post Abortion-Syndrome: The Solution in Search of a Problem," Huffington Post, August 12, 2013, www.huffingtonpost.com/sarah-erdreich/post-abortionsyndrome-the_b_3742606.html.

7.   "Mental Health Issues and Abortion."

8.   "AAAS Board Resolution on Intelligent Design Theory," *American Association for the Advancement of Science*, October 18, 2002, http://tinyurl.com/pzr8n3z.

9.   "Mental Health Issues and Abortion."

10.   "Abortion and Mental Health: Evaluating the Evidence," *American Psychologist* 64, no. 9 (December 2009): 866–85, http://www.apa.org/pubs/journals/features/amp-64-9-863.pdf.

11.   "Neonatal Death," March of Dimes, 2010, www.marchofdimes.com/loss/neonatal-death.aspx; G. H. Breborowicz,

"Limits of Fetal Viability and Its Enhancement," *Early Pregnancy* 5, no. 1 (January 2001), www.ncbi.nlm.nih.gov/pubmed/11753511.

12. Friedman and Dolansky, *The Bible Now*, 42.

13. Gerald and Kathleen Hill, "Murder," in *The People's Law Dictionary* (Publisher Fine Communications), dictionary.law.com/Default.aspx?selected=1303.

14. "World Abortion Policies 2013," United Nations, Department of Economic and Social Affairs, Population Division, http://tinyurl.com/n4h2sz6 (accessed September 17, 2014).

15. Drorag O'Donnell Setel, "Abortion," in *The Oxford Guide to the Bible* (New York: Oxford University Press, 1993), 4.

16. Friedman and Dolansky, *The Bible Now*, 44.

17. Friedman and Dolansky, *The Bible Now*, 50.

18. Friedman and Dolansky, *The Bible Now*, 52.

19. Carr, *Annotated*, 13–14.

20. Rasha Dabash and Farzaneh Roudi-Fahimi, "Abortion in the Middle East and North Africa," *PBS*, September 2008, pbs.org/publications/reports.2008/abortion-mena.aspx.

21. George Devereaux, "Typological Study of Abortion in 350 Primitive, Ancient, and Pre-industrial Societies," in *Abortion in America: Medical, Psychiatric, Legal, Anthropological, and Religious Considerations* (Boston: Beacon Press, 1967), 97–152.

22. J. Robert Sallares, "Abortion," in *Oxford Classical Dictionary*, 3rd ed. (New York: Oxford University Press, 2003).

23. Eugene S. McCartney, "Sex Determination and Control in Antiquity," *American Journal of Philology* 43, no. 1 (1922): 62–70.

24. Aristotle, *On the Generation of Animals*, Book II, updated, https://ebooks.adelaide.edu.au/a/aristotle/generation/book2.html (accessed September 17, 2014).

25. Jonathan A. Draper, "The Apostolic Fathers: The Didache," *Expository Times* 117, no. 5 (2006): 177–81.

26.   Bart D. Ehrman, *Lost Scriptures: Books That Did Not Make It into the New Testament* (New York: Oxford University Press, 2003), 284.

27.   Ehrman, *Lost Scriptures*, 234, 284.

28.   Pagels, *Serpent*, 29.

29.   J. Walker, J. Sheppard, and H. Browne, *Nicene and Post-Nicene Fathers*, First Series, vol. 11, ed. Philip Schaff, revised by George B. Stevens (Buffalo: Christian Literature Publishing Co., 1889), http://www.newadvent.org/fathers/210224.htm.

30.   Katherine Brind'Amour, "St. Thomas Aquinas," Embryo Project Encyclopedia, Arizona State University, November 11, 2007, https://embryo.asu.edu/pages/st-thomas-aquinas-c-1225-1274 (accessed July 19, 2014).

31.   William E. May, "Abortion and Ensoulment: Augustine and Aquinas vs. Pelosi and Biden, Part I," Culture of Life Foundation, September 16, 2008, http://www.culture-of-life.org/2008/09/16/abortion-and-ensoulment-augustine-and-aquinas-vs-pelosi-and-biden-part-i/.

32.   Daniel C. Maguire, *Sacred Rights: The Case for Contraception and Abortion in World Religions* (New York: Oxford University Press, 2003), 88.

33.   Sehat, *Myth*, 261–62.

34.   Sehat, *Myth*, 265–66.

35.   Sehat, *Myth*, 268.

36.   Sehat, *Myth*, 281.

37.   For more, see Hedges, *American Fascists*, 23, 61, 84–85, 92, 109, 138–39.

4

Homosexuality, Transgenderism, and Transsexuality

As a start to this chapter, I should clarify why I included these three separate topics together. Indeed, people may identify as gay, transgender, or transsexual, or as gay, transgender, and transsexual, or as some combination of the three. As these groups are not mutually exclusive, some overlap can occur, but my intention is not to suggest that the three groups are always directly connected. Rather, I've grouped them together here because the prejudice against and assumptions about each of these groups stem from a common history.

The Human Rights Campaign reports that hate crimes against LGBTQ individuals account for roughly 14 percent of all hate crimes reported by the FBI, the third highest of any category. Studies conducted by the National Gay and Lesbian Task Force Policy Institute have found that 44 percent of LGBT individuals have reported facing discrimination in the workplace, and 32 percent have faced discrimination when renting a place to live. Many individuals also report having experienced discrimination in restaurants and educational systems, and when receiving health care and getting insurance.[1] A study by the Equal Rights Center and Freedom to Work found that LGBT applicants for federal contracting jobs are 23 percent less likely to be called back for an interview, even if another applicant is less qualified than the LGBT candidate.[2]

The Centers for Disease Control and Prevention reports that homophobia, the stigma against the lifestyle and practice of homosexuality, limits gay men's access to quality health care that is responsive to their health needs. The same stigma also affects their income levels, employment status, and their ability to not only receive health care, but also maintain their health care coverage. As a direct result, this negatively contributes to their mental health and leads to substance abuse, risky sexual behavior, and suicide. Negative views of homosexuality also make it difficult for people who are gay to be open about their sexuality with those close to them, further heightening stress, limiting social support, and, again, adversely affecting health. Due to the strong stigma, gay men are 8.4 times more likely to attempt suicide, 5.9 times more likely to report high levels of depression, 3.4 times more likely to abuse substances, and 3.4 times more likely to engage in risky sexual activity.[3]

It is not just in public businesses, hospitals, and the work force where LGBTQ individuals encounter discrimination.

In the most extreme cases, they also face persecution far beyond being denied a job, health care, or a meal. In 1998, for example, the brutal killing of Matthew Shepard made international headlines. He was beaten, tortured, tied to a fence, and left to die.[4] Doctors determined the trauma was so severe they could not successfully operate on him.[5] Nearly two decades later, horrific anti-LGBTQ attacks continue. In 2014 a man reportedly killed two gay men in Seattle after finding them using a social networking app.[6] In Texas, a man killed his daughter and her lesbian lover because he did not like that she was gay,[7] while another man in Texas shot a lesbian couple, killing one and severely injuring the other.[8] In South Africa, a 21-year-old man was tied up, beaten, and set on fire because he was gay.[9] A man in Glasgow, Scotland, stabbed his wife twelve times after discovering messages on her iPad between her and her girlfriend.[10] In California, a 15-year-old boy was shot to death by a 14-year-old classmate when he came out as gay.[11] In 2003, a transgender woman in Indianapolis was murdered by a man after he discovered she was not a cisgender woman (a woman whose gender identity matches her societally recognized sex),[12] and in 2009 a man was sentenced to life in prison for killing a transgender woman he met on a social networking site.[13]

As I hope to have demonstrated, anti-LGBTQ sentiment is a hugely important issue with grave effects. People are so filled with hate they are willing not only to inflict harm—but also to do it in the most severe and barbaric ways imaginable. A lot of this intense animosity toward homosexuality, transgenderism, and transsexuality stems from certain religious fundamentalist beliefs—specifically, that the Bible says that these lifestyles or practices are sinful and contrary to the teachings of God and Jesus. However, what we shall discover looking into such fundamentalist beliefs is that nothing could be further from the truth.

What Does the Bible Say?

One of the most commonly cited biblical passages by anti-gay advocates is Leviticus 18:22, "You shall not lie with a male as with a woman; it is an abomination." Taken at face value, sure, this line would seem to imply a prohibition against, at the very least, male-on-male homosexual acts. But looking at the overall context of this chapter suggests another meaning to the passage.

Leviticus 18:18 states, "You shall not take a woman [as a wife] as a rival to her sister, uncovering her nakedness while her sister is still alive." This is the closest we come to seeing anything remotely suggesting sexual relations between women. Yet, this passage does not say at all that a woman lying with a woman is prohibited; rather, it says that a man is prohibited from having sex with a woman if he is already married to her sister.

Elsewhere in Leviticus 18 we find prohibitions against intercourse with another person's wife. (Recall the earlier discussion about women as property.) Verse 21, meanwhile, reads, "You shall not give any of your offspring to sacrifice them to Molech, and so profane the name of your God: I am your Lord." So, right among the laws against lying with the sister of one's wife, and lying with men as with women, we have a law prohibiting not child sacrifice, but child sacrifice to the Canaanite god, Molech.

What is noteworthy is that in Leviticus 18:22—and in Leviticus 20:13, which says that a man who lies with a man as with a woman "shall surely be put to death"—the Hebrew word used for "abomination" is *to'eba*. Each time this word is used in the Hebrew Bible, it is used to link an action with worship of a foreign deity. So, much like sacrificing a child to Molech is an act of profaning the name of God, so too is male-on-male sexuality an abomination. The acts themselves are not the main issue. Rather, the implication of such acts—that they denote the worship of a foreign deity—is the problem.[14] Consider Leviticus 18:24–25, which says, "for by all these practices the nations I am casting out before you [the Canaanites, who inhabited Israel, the promised land, prior to the Israelites] have defiled themselves. Thus the land became defiled; and I punished it for its iniquity, and the land vomited out its inhabitants." A similar idea is shared in 1 Kings 14:24: "they did according to all the abominations of the nations which Yahweh drove out before the children of Israel." Further, *to'eba* is used very frequently as part of a sort of stock phrase that reads *to'eba ha-goyim*, which means "the uncleanliness of the Gentiles." This phrase is used in 2 Kings 16:3, as well as in the aforementioned 1 Kings passage.[15] In this regard, then, the act of male-on-male intercourse is truly a secondary issue. The authors of Leviticus 18:22 and 20:13 were concerned that, by participating in homoeroticism, individuals were resorting to practices carried out by the Canaanites and worshipping Canaanite gods.

Anti-gay religious fundamentalists also frequently cite the story of Sodom and Gomorrah, from Genesis 19:1–11. As it is commonly alleged, the city was so full of sin from the practice of homoeroticism that the townspeople attempted to sodomize (a term derived from this story) the two angels who visited Lot. If we look at chapters surrounding this one, we find that the original biblical authors did not in any way intend to suggest a prohibition against or punishment for homosexual practices. In Genesis 13:12, for example, when Yahweh approaches Abraham about the inhabitants of Sodom and Gomorrah, he says they are sinful, but does not explicitly say what they did to be labeled as sinful. So, by the time God sends the angels to visit Lot, he has already determined that the people there are sinful. More to the point, he has decided to destroy the city *before* any threat of rape to the angels. It is actually not until the book of Ezekiel that we find any mention of the inhabitants' crimes. It says, at 16:49, "Behold, this was the iniquity of thy sister, Sodom, pride, fulness of bread, and abundance of idleness was in her and in her daughters, neither did she strengthen the hand of the poor and needy." According to the Bible itself, therefore, Sodom and Gomorrah were guilty of pride, uncharitableness, greed, and, ultimately, xenophobia, for the hostility shown toward the visiting strangers.[16] Ecclesiastes (16:8) and the Book of Wisdom (19:13–14) both say Sodom was punished for the inhabitants' pride as well.

Looking back at the original story of Sodom and Gomorrah, it is important to note the language used and its context. In Hebrew, as in certain other languages, when people are in a group, the group is refered to in the masculine form as long as at least one man is in the group. The word used in Hebrew for the mob that goes to Lot's house is '*anasim*, which is the masculine plural of man, or person, and occurs a total of twenty-one times in Genesis alone. In this context, the word actually means "people" and not "men." To assume that only men went to Lot's house demanding to "know" the angels shows a lack of understanding of the language.

Further, assuming for a moment this story has any basis in reality, the idea that Lot and his family would be the only straight members of a city defies everything we know about human sexuality.[17] It should also be noted that God destroyed two other cities, Admah and Zeboim, along with Sodom and Gomorrah. So, this would mean then that Lot and his family were the only heterosexual individuals of not just two but four different cities.[18] As a point of comparison, an estimated 2.3 percent of the current U.S. population identifies as gay, lesbian, or bisexual.[19] The logical questions presented by such a scenario are thus legion.

In Judges 19:22 we find a story that is almost a direct parallel to this one. A man comes to a new city and is offered a place to stay in a nice man's home. The next morning, a crowd gathers at the door demanding to "know" the stranger who has come into their village. Again, the word *'anasim* is used here, indicating that it is a crowd of both men and women. As with Lot's story in Genesis, the master of the house offers his virgin daughter to the angry mob, whom they reject. Instead, they take the stranger's concubine, ". . . and they knew her, and abused her all the night until the morning: and when the day began to spring, they let her go." Even more appalling than the rape and abuse of the concubine is the stranger's reaction the next day. After finding her unconscious outside, he tells her to get going. When she does not respond, "he took a knife, and laid hold on his concubine, and divided her, together with her bones, into twelve pieces, and sent her into all the coasts of Israel." So, in this story, the city is not destroyed, and the people realize their violent impulses, with no punishment from God. Yet, according to present-day religious moralizers, we are to believe that, despite these nearly identical stories, the problem is homosexuality.

So what then is going on with all the instances of gang rape? Well, rape is an act of power and dominance over others. As history well attests, this is something that is not unique to the Israelites or to the Bible, let alone the two stories mentioned here. Sexual acts, even violent ones, demonstrated virility, masculinity, and strength. This is why the patriarchs of the Abrahamic faiths have so many wives and concubines. Solomon, as we have noted, had 700 wives and 300 concubines. Such an assembly symbolized not only his wealth, as women had a bride price, but also his power. But, more than that, it showed the power that *men* had over women. To be penetrated meant to be feminized—to be submissive to another.[20] In ancient warfare, the winners would not uncommonly anally penetrate the losers to demonstrate their dominance over them. In an ancient Greek painting depicting the victory of Athens over the Persians by the River Eurymedon in 460 BCE, a Persian is bent over, attempting to fight off a Greek soldier with an erect phallus in his hand. The caption reads, "I am Eurymedon. I have bent down."[21] So, in this context, anal rape represented an expression of submission and dominance.

The closest we see to anything regarding transgenderism or transsexuality in the Bible is at Deuteronomy 22:5: "A woman shall not wear that which pertains to a man, neither shall a man put on a woman's garment; for whosoever does these things is an abomination to Yahweh your God." There is that word "abomination" again. And, very much like the practice of male-on-male intercourse, wearing clothing not attributed to the "proper" gender was something that other cultures practiced. So, to differentiate the Israelites from the Canaanites, who God so hated that he vomited them out of the land, the Israelites were not permitted to do such things. The same can be said of castration, which was similarly a sign of worship to foreign gods (for more, see the next chapter). Aside from the aforementioned passages, Bible verses such as Ezra 9:10, Nehemiah 13:23-31, and Malachi 2:11-12 also show an abandonment of religious and cultural practices that were specific to other cultures.[22]

Interestingly, the Hebrew Bible offers no prohibitions against same-sex relations in those sections where you would expect such prohibitions to occur if God were especially concerned about this practice. This includes the Covenant Code, in Exodus 21–23, the J Decalogue, in Exodus 34:14–26, and the Deuteronomic Law Code (12–26). It is also interesting that the Bible is consistently concerned about the worship of false idols—so much so that it even prohibits the eating of shellfish—yet the prohibitions against homosexuality occur only in the priestly laws and holiness code in Leviticus. That is due, in part, to the priestly authors being close to the monarchy and concerned with the purity of the lineage of Israel.[23]

Outside of the Hebrew Bible, we see mention of homosexuality in Romans 1:26–27: "God gave them over to shameful lusts. Even their women exchanged natural sexual relations for unnatural ones. In the same way the men also abandoned natural relations with women and were inflamed with lust for one another. Men committed shameful acts with other men." On its surface, this passage approaches a prohibition, but we need to look at, once again, the language used and how it was used to understand what message Paul intended to communicate. To begin, the Greek word he uses for "unnatural" is *paraphysin*, which does not so much translate as "unnatural" but, more appropriately, as "severely unconventional." Consider how Seneca, a Roman statesman who lived and worked in the same period as Paul, felt that hot baths, potted plants, and banquets after sunset were all *contra naturam*, or against nature.[24] In contrast, also consider what Paul sees as "natural"—for example, he states that, by nature, Jews are uncircumcised (Romans 2:27); a Jew is a Jew by nature (Galatians 2:15); and by the light of nature, people can do what the law requires (Romans 2:14).

Looking at the passage in context to the rest of the chapter, we see something similar to what we found in the Leviticus passage. In Romans 1:21–22, Paul writes, "For although they knew God, they neither glorified him as God nor gave thanks to him, but their thinking became futile and their foolish hearts were darkened. Although they claimed to be wise, they became fools." A verse or two later, Paul writes how these individuals were given over, by God, to "sexual impurity for the degrading of their bodies with one another." So, very much like the Leviticus passage, the act of homoeroticism is secondary to what the act implies—namely, that the people participating in the practice are worshipping false idols. Paul is less concerned with homosexuality and more concerned with people not worshipping the God of Israel. Of course, Paul also wished that everyone would be abstinent as he was (1 Corinthians 7:8–9), so it might be easy to see why he would equate any form of sexual practice with not preparing one's self for the coming kingdom of God on earth.

Maybe it is easy to write off further writings of Paul with this in mind, but let us continue to look at what he said, as some of his passages are interpreted as referring to homoerotic practices, but, in fact, make no such reference. 1 Corinthians 6:9, for example, says that "men who have sex with men" are among a list of other sinners who will not inherit the kingdom of God. A similar reference to those who practice homosexuality appears in 1 Timothy 1:10. But the words used are the Greek *malakoi* and *arsenokoitai*, and a few problems arise when translating these words as "men who practice homoeroticism."

First, *arsenokoitai* is an incredibly rare Greek word, especially in Paul's letters. It is a very literal translation from the Hebrew *miskab zakur*, meaning "lying with men." The Septuagint, the Greek translation of the Hebrew Bible, at Leviticus 20:13, uses the term *arsenos koiten*, which actually refers to male prostitutes, but not to male prostitutes who sleep only with men. These male prostitutes were known to sleep with both genders. As for *malakoi*, the term simply referred to someone who was soft, or graceful; it stressed femininity, but did not imply homosexuality.[25] It might be used today as a synonym for "callow"; in fact, up through the Reformation, Catholics thought that the term applied to masturbation. The words are never used to reference homosexual people or acts. They are, much like the Leviticus passage, in reference to heterosexual people doing things, and not necessarily sexual things, that implied practicing pagan rituals or worshipping pagan gods. As we see a verse later, in 1 Corinthians 6:10, those labeled as *arsenokoitai* are lumped together with "thieves, the greedy, drunkards, revilers, [and] robbers"—all Gentiles, or non-Jews, being proselytized to by Paul.[26]

As Michael Coogan writes, "I suspect that Paul was informed in part by the ancient Israelite taboo against mixing categories, a concept found elsewhere in his letters ... it was too culturally conditioned, as was his insistence that men should not wear their hair long because to do so was unnatural."[27] With regard to the literalist idea that the Bible prohibits homosexuality, he adds, "when [contemporary moralists] appeal to the Bible's authority as a timeless and absolute moral code, they ignore the cultural contexts in which the Bible was written."[28]

Outside of the Bible

There are numerous stories from antiquity showing a positive relationship between same-sex individuals, both fictional and historical. Homosexual intercourse is described in art from Uruk, Assur, Babylon, and Susa from as far back as the third millennium BCE.[29] In ancient Egypt, Seth and Horus had homoerotic relations with no negative repercussions. The Book of the Dead had people recite, "I haven't had sex with boys," but it does not speak any more on the matter. Relations with young boys may have been frowned upon, but there were no laws that indicate same-sex relations were illegal or looked at unfavorably.[30] There is also the story of Gilgamesh and Enkindu from Mesopotamia. In the story, Gilgamesh covers Enkindu's body "like a bride" and declines the goddess Ishtar's advances. We also see a similar story with Achilles and Patroclus in the Illiad, which mirrors a similar relationship in the Hebrew Bible's story of Jonathan and King David.[31] So, already, we are seeing a historically positive idea of homoerotic relations, at least in terms of literature and well-known stories.

As for the real world, we find anti-gay laws in Middle Assyria. One, for example, states that a man who penetrates a male friend would as punishment be raped by "them" (presumably the community) and castrated. A man who has sex with another man's wife would be punished in a similar fashion. It should be noted, however, that these particular laws are reflective of acts committed between social equals (*tappa'u*). If social equals were caught in the act, the submissive partner would be viewed as having been raped, and the punishment would go to the active partner. This was because, in a situation between social equals, the act of penetration would represent securing dominion over the other, causing the submissive partner to lose his status as a social equal.[32]

Far from being outlawed, the practice of pederasty was an accepted practice in ancient Greece. Pederasty comes from the Greek *pederastia*, meaning "love for boys." In various ancient periods, it was a practice that was seen as a "right of passage" for all males and viewed as *the* way for men to become full-fledged members of Greek society, or *agoge*. Sparta actually believed that "only lovers can die for one another" and had its troops arranged to keep those in pederastic relationships close. (This should make you view things differently when watching *300* again.) Plato even stated, in *Symposium* and *Phaedrus*, that he felt the city would be easier to rule and control with pederastic relations. He wrote, "Pederasty was noblest of all human relations . . . [it is the] purest of love."[33]

Participants in these pederastic relationships were not "gay" in the modern understanding of the term. In fact, the Hebrew, Greek, Aramaic, and Syriac languages had no word that meant "homosexual" the way that we know the term today. Even today, Hebrew and Arabic have no word that equates to our understanding of the word "gay" or "homosexual." In fact, the term "homosexual" did not exist until the 19th century.[34] According to ancient Greek tradition, sex was not a regular part of pederastic relationships. In fact, sex did not usually happen at all, depending on whether you view penetration as a necessary part of sex. The physical part of the relationship involved "intercrural" contact, meaning nonpenetrative and nonmutual manual stimulation between the thighs. Part of this was due to the idea that sexual pleasure was to be had by the dominant participant only. If the passive partner received pleasure, it only strengthened the concept that the passive partner was weak.[35]

Suffice it to say, homoeroticism was a regular part of Greek culture. We see it in ancient Greek writings and art, but, even in nonpederastic contexts, it was not homosexuality in the modern sense. Rather, it might be more appropriately called "institutionalized bisexuality." While homoerotic romances were legal and socially acknowledged, this did not mean men in such romances partook only in homoerotic relationships. Due to the lack of medical knowledge and means that we have today, infant mortality rates were high and women died regularly in childbirth. Each family had to have five children simply to *maintain* the population. But marriage was not a relationship entered out of love; it was more of a business transaction to ensure progeny, wealth, and land expansion or retention.[36] Thus, men involved in same-sex romantic relationships also had wives and families.

Roman society of the time had much in common with the Greeks when it came to homoeroticism. In fact, for the first two hundred years of Roman rule, the emperors in power were mostly individuals who enjoyed, or preferred, same-sex romantic encounters.[37] This included Nero, who had male lovers, and Hadrian, who had a boyfriend named Antonius.[38] Poets, like Catullus, Martial, and Tibullus, wrote of homoerotic relations between freed men. For example, Catullus wrote poetry about a relationship he had with another man.[39] Martial wrote poems detailing the emperor's relations with a boy named Earinos, and Minucius Felix, an early Christian apologist, wrote that gay relations were "the Roman religion."[40]

Although documents exist in which citizens oppose or speak out against homoeroticism, they never cite any laws that would suggest such opposition was based on any legal ideals. As an example, Cicero wrote that homoerotic relations were *contra mas*, or against good mores, and, despite blaming the Greeks for the practice, never refers to any laws to advocate for his position.[41] He even wrote that, even though he did not like the practice, "*Quod non crimen est*" ("This is not a crime").[42] In contrast, Valerius Maximus wrote that a boy in Rome had been tried for adultery with a married woman, under a law that protected Roman citizens from sexual violence, but he was set free after testifying that he was in the room out of passion for another man.[43] In his testimony, he freely admitted to homosexual acts and stated he had been with a male prostitute at the time. Not only were his actions perfectly legal, but also the idea of male prostitutes was well known, as they paid taxes to the empire and even had their own vacation day on April 26 of each year.[44] The fact remains, neither Roman religion nor law viewed homoerotic practices as inferior to or unmistakable from heterosexuality.

Contrary to the Greeks, the Romans found no romance in homoeroticism, especially in regard to taking the passive role. Male citizens relied on their slaves for sexual release before marriage. In addition, prior to becoming married, they would "practice" for their wedding night on their male slaves, and the more wealthy occupants of Rome could afford most slaves to practice on. Martial even wrote in complaint to a friend who would not lend him a male slave for sexual purposes. But, as mentioned, the Romans were prejudiced against individuals who were typically in the passive role in erotic encounters. Aside from women, this also included boys and slaves, all of whom were excluded from the public power structure. Julius Caesar even wrote of his displeasure for Nicomedes, the king of Bithynia, due to the rumors that circulated that he was sexually passive to other men.[45]

Even so, same-sex marriages were commonplace and legal. Cicero, though not in favor of gay relationships, regarded Curio's relationship with another man a marriage. In Lampridius, Elagabalus wrote that, after the emperor married an athlete from Smyrna, any male who wished to advance at the imperial court had to have a husband or pretend that he did. Juvenal and Martial also wrote of public gay marriage ceremonies, which included the families of the couples, dowries, and legal niceties. Nero even married two male couples in succession in public ceremonies, which included rituals common to heterosexual marriages and were just as legal as male-female nuptials.[46]

As for women, same-sex relations between them were also known and tolerated if not accepted in various periods and places in the ancient world. No laws existed against sexual relationships between women in Mesopotamia,[47] and we have references to women who participated in homoerotic practices in the Partheneion songs of Alcman, a Spartan songwriter, or choral poet, in the sixth century BCE.[48] In this period prior to the era of Plato and Aristotle, when gender identification and roles had a much more strict definition in society, women also did things in Greece that would be viewed by today's standards as being rather masculine. For example, a woman named Sappho had a gym on the island of Lesbos that was similar to the ones Greek men used.

Despite these seemingly accepting views toward homoerotic behavior by women, sexual relationships between women would eventually come to be seen as an unfavorable practice. The women of Lesbos became examples of shameful behavior and the term *lesbiazein* ("to act like a person from Lesbos") was used disparagingly to refer to people who were flirtatious and performed fellatio. Note the association between women performing romantic acts with other women and a sexual act performed on men. As the Greek *Oneirokritika* (Interpretation of Dreams) described, woman-on-woman sexual acts were regarded as *paraphysin*, or "against nature," as were acts such as self-fellatio, oral copulation, and bestiality.[49]

Pieces of Roman literature equated female same-sex relations to a married woman committing adultery, as it was unnatural for women to attempt to take on the active role in intercourse. Rome viewed the active partner as assuming the "male" position in sex, called *tribas*. Seneca (4–64 CE) wrote that women practicing same-sex activities "even rival men in their lusts . . . although [they] burn to be passive."[50] Seneca thought that, if a woman should be caught by her husband in a same-sex lovemaking act, she should be put to death.[51] Martial, in *Bassa* 1:90, showed disgust for female same-sex relations. A woman he once praised for being "chaste" and uninterested in men eventually became, in his eyes, a *fututor*, which is an obscenity for male sexual activity. Philaenis, who behaved in a "macho" way, preferred the active role during her sexual encounters and claimed that fellatio was not "manly enough" for her. Wrote Martial, "Pricks she won't suck; she thinks it's sissy, but gobbles up the cracks of girls. Philaenis, may the gods bestow what you think butch—a cunt to lick."[52]

With regard to transsexual and transgendered individuals in the ancient world, we have records of them as well. In Mesopotamia, the *assinnu, kugarru,* and *kulu'u* were male members of a religious movement who worked under the honor of Ishtar who dressed as females. Part of their life-long devotion involved castration. Mesopotamia even had places in public and military offices for such individuals, eunuchs called *sha-reshi*. Emasculated priests known as *galli* worshipped the Syrian goddess Atargatis, the Mediterranean "Great Mother," Cybele, and Cybele's companion, Attis, who was said to have died of self-emasculation. They may also have taken part in sexual acts as the passive partner to connect to the goddess.[53]

Similar to the *assinnu* were the Indian *hijras*, who were male anatomically but dressed as women, performed an emasculation ritual, and took a passive role in sex with men.[54] Romans had a similar classification for men, called the *cinaedi*, who worked as prostitutes and dressed as women. In this manner, they took on a passive sexual role, but they were specifically not castrated. Juvenal wrote about them in *Satire VI*, detailing how they had formed a subculture with a fixed form of social behavior.[55] Even though many of these individuals were straight in their personal lives, they received hostility due to their reputation for promiscuity and debauchery.[56]

So What Happened?

The first point to understand, when analyzing views toward homosexuality across time and space, is that almost no early Christians appealed to Leviticus as an authority against homosexual acts.[57] Similarly, early Christians did not cite the story of Sodom and Gomorrah to condemn homosexual fornication. The earliest Christian reference to the story's punishment is found in the Epistle of Jude (1:7). There, the described punishment is for fornication, not homosexual fornication. After all, when Jude was written, the crime in the story was believed to have been *women* having intercourse with angels.[58] If we look at the preceding verse, Jude links Sodom and Gomorrah with the flood story in Genesis. Genesis 6:4 refers to the Nephilim, the sons of God (or angels), having intercourse with human women, which in turn brings God's judgment to humanity. Since God later places his bow in the sky to show his promise that he would never decimate the human population again (Genesis 9:13), for future such cases,

God's best course of action was to destroy the villages and punish the people guilty of those same sins.

The second point to keep in mind is that people looking at the Bible in later generations, including the authors of the New Testament books, worked with mistranslations. Even Paul of Tarsus, who seemed well versed in Hebrew scripture, likely used the Septuagint, the Greek translation, as he was a Greek-speaking citizen. There is no indication that Paul had any training in the rabbinic tradition. Thus, when he did quote scripture, he would have quoted or paraphrased the Septuagint.[59] One example of such mistranslations is "sodomite," a word mistranslated from the Hebrew *kadash* or *kadashim*. In a previous chapter, I referenced the practice of ritualized orgies, performed by sacred prostitutes, in the Solomonic Temple in Jerusalem to honor the pagan goddess Asherah.[60] The word *kadash* refers to male and female cult prostitutes and *kadashim* means "hallowed" or "sacred." Neither word denotes a sexual orientation, let alone a gender. The Septuagint actually translated the terms in six different ways. One instance misrepresented the gender of the individual, but none of these translations hinted at homosexuality or homoeroticism. Later, the Latin Vulgate furthered the problem by translating the words as "effeminite" and even "scuratator," which implicated homosexuality. It was not until the Hebrew Bible was translated into English, many centuries later, that the word(s) would condemn homoerotic behavior.[61]

Josephus, in *Antiquities* 1:194–204, interpreted the story of Sodom and Gomorrah as a prohibition against homosexuality. He boasted that the Jews were proudly homophobic, while criticizing Mark Antony in *Antiquities* 15:28–29 for his "love of boys."[62] Cicero wrote the same of Antony, stating, "You took up the toga for males, which you immediately converted that into a woman."[63] Philo of Alexandria also looked down on homoeroticism, calling it a "fatal woman's illness" and stating that it destroyed semen, led to infertility or sterility, and even gave the partners venereal disease. Further, he believed that it made boys women, that procreation was the only real reason to perform any erotic acts,[64] and that any sexual act that could not result in children was against nature. Of course, he also believed celibacy, masturbation, and failure to divorce a barren wife were unnatural as well.[65]

Tacitus, in his *Annals* (15:44),[66] actually objected to Christianity, as did Pliny the Younger (*Epistles* 10.96), for Christianity's "sexual loosness."[67] In fact, people like John Chrysostom (347–407 CE) admitted that practices like homoeroticism were rampant in Christian circles. An apologetics piece by Minucius Felix in *Octavius* included reference to ceremonial fellatio and temple prostitution.[68] It was not until asceticism, or the practice of abstinence, be it of sex, vices, or living a comfortable life (think the life of Jesus, the apostles, and John the Baptist), provided backing to opposition for homoeroticism that the oppression of homosexuality really took hold. This was partially thanks to the apocryphal Epistle of Barnabas.

The Epistle of Barnabas is a Greek religious text likely written somewhere between 70 and 130 CE—that is, somewhere between the destruction of the Jerusalem Temple in 70 CE and the Bar Kochba Revolt of 132 CE. This time frame is generally accepted because it mentions, at 16:3–4, the destruction of the Temple and notes that the servants of the enemy (the Romans) would help rebuild the Temple, which likely did not occur after the revolt. Clement, Origen, and Eusebius cite this epistle in their writings. The epistle states, "Moses said you shall not eat the hare [Leviticus 11:5] . . . you may not become a boy-molester." While this line is antagonistic toward homosexuals presuming, as many do today, that homosexuals molest children, it suffers from a mistranslation. The Greek word translated as "boy-molester" is *paidophthoros*, which actually means "child-molester" and implies either gender. Despite this, the Epistle of Barnabas, once thought of as canonical, helped place a target on the backs of those who engaged in homosexual acts.[69] This rule against homosexual sex, or sex not intended for procreation, later became known as the "Alexandrian rule," thanks to Clement of Alexandria in his *Paedogogu*.[70] Novatian, a third-century CE theologian and priest who had a Latin translation of the epistle, equated homosexuality with gender confusion, writing, "What does [the] law intend . . . it condemns those men who have made themselves women." Such ideas and associations, in turn, affected perceptions of homosexuality to an absurd degree.[71]

Theologian and philosopher Augustine of Hippo (354–430 CE) wrote, in Sermo 2.235 and "Homilia" in *Hexaemeron* 9.6, that husbands, if unable to control their passions, should perform "unnatural" sexual acts only with prostitutes. This, of course, showed he was either not aware of or ignored Paul of Tarsus' prohibition against the use of prostitutes, in 1 Corinthians 6:15–20. When saying an act was *contra naturam*, or against nature, both Paul and Augustine meant the act was uncharacteristic or unideal—and not literally against a law of nature, as modern moralists interpret the term today. While Augustine never compares homoerotic acts to heterosexual ones, he does declare that procreation is the only *moral* use of sexuality.[72]

The Greek word *arsenokoitai,* which we have already become familiar with, was initially used with no negative connotation. This changed, however, in the fourth century CE, as theocracy took over the empire, thanks to Severus Alexander. People could no longer choose a religion, job, or home without the direct influence of imperial authority. This included limitations on sexual expression and religious practices. Even the *exoleti*, or male prostitutes who took the active position (as opposed to *catamiti*, or male prostitutes who took the passive position), were persecuted by Alexander, principally through taxation, which drove much of the prostitution underground. While Alexander's successor, Philip, eventually outlawed male prostitutes in the Western Roman Empire, prostitution, or at least male prostitution, was not abolished across the entire empire until the sixth century CE. Evidence of its abolition is found in the jurist Paulus' work *Sententiae,* which says that a man hired an *exoleti* prostitute and ended up losing half of his estate as a result.[73]

Gay marriage was officially outlawed in the Western Roman Empire in 342 CE and, in 390, Emperor Theodosius started implementing corporeal punishment for homoerotic acts. Though Theodosius felt homosexuality was horrendous, his views did not reflect that of the general public. It should be noted that he also inflicted death sentences for things like pagan idol worship, which was legal prior to and for centuries after Theodosius' reign. This changing treatment of homosexuality came with the rise of power of the Church, which began with Constantine a few decades prior and contributed to a higher value placed on moral absolutes.

In the Eastern Roman Empire, or Byzantine Empire, Emperor Justinian is recorded as having castrated two bishops in the sixth century, Isaiah of Rhodes and Alexander of Diospolis, for homoerotic activities. Theophanes writes, in *Chronography*, "the bishops . . . were deposed from office, as having been discovered to be lovers of boys, and were punished frightfully by the emperor, having their male organs cut off."[74] This punishment occurred prior to any such law being put in place in the Byzantine Empire, and the views held by Justinian were not held by rulers of neighboring imperial cities. As an example, Procopius, a scholar who worked alongside Justinian, said laws against minorities were used outside of Byzantium to obtain money from them. This included not only those who practiced homosexual acts, but also Samaritans, pagans, unorthodox Christians, and astrologers. But Justinian was not alone in his distaste for homosexuals, as his wife, Theodora, also attempted to persecute those caught in homoerotic acts. Unfortunately for her, the judges refused to hear the charges and the city ended up celebrating a holiday in honor of those who were accused.[75]

The following century, in Spain, the Visigoths, branches of the nomadic tribes of Germanic people, passed legislation that dictated homosexuality was punishable by castration. This law was largely due to the Visigoths becoming Catholic in 589. The Visigoths' legislation, which included punishment of Jews, was done primarily to endorse conformity among the people of Spain. Despite the speaking out by people like Isidore of Seville and Toledo IV, an unarmed clergy was no match for the barbarism of the Visigoths. As a result, hostility and antagonism grew toward homosexuality.[76]

Various religious leaders offered penance for homosexual acts, like Pope Gregory IV and Regino of Prum. Some did not feel it was as wicked or sinful as heterosexual infidelity with a married man, as Burchard, bishop of Worms, believed. Even Pope Leo IX forbade extreme measures in dealing with homosexuality, at least among the clergy. But this relaxed attitude toward homosexuality within the Church did not last. In 1102, the Council of London decreed that sodomy should be confessed as a sin. The third Lateran Council in 1179 declared that "whoever shall be found to have committed that incontinence which is against nature, on account of which the wrath of God came upon the sons of perdition and consumed five cities with fire, shall, if a cleric, be deposed from office or confined to a monastery to do penance; if a layman, he shall suffer excommunication and be cast out from the company of the faithful."[77]

Such rulings were in part a reflection of European views after the first Crusades. Stories circulated about Muslim women and their daughters singing lewd songs and Muslim men who raped men "of every age" and even bishops. Paralleling the made-up story of William of Norwich, a Christian boy said to have been crucified by Jews to further antagonize a group that did not conform to Christian ideals, these stories, which often involved the violation of young children, were similarly made up to make villains out of a group. Outside of the common folklore of the day, the official accounts never document any such event, neither the crucifixion of a young boy by Jews, nor the rape of men of every age, even bishops, by Muslims.[78]

In the thirteenth century, there was a massive alteration to the legal structure in Europe that spelled out a loss of freedom for disadvantaged social groups, including homosexuals, Jews, and the poor. They were cited as the cause of social unrest and became the object of legislation and antipathy.[79] From this came the Castilian Royal Edict, which stated, if two men were caught in a homosexual act, they were to be castrated before a crowd and hung by the legs until they died, never to have their bodies taken down. This was the first time a European law had deemed an action to be "against nature."[80] In France, according to the legal school of Orleans, the punishment for the first offense of a homosexual sex act was castration, dismemberment for the second, and immolation for the third. For female homosexual acts, the punishment was dismemberment for the first two offenses.[81] Informed by Thomas Aquinas' writing and the views of early church fathers—that all nonprocreative acts were against nature— medieval European attitudes toward homosexuality had finally reached a point reflected in today's most anti-gay societies.[82] The faith had authoritatively condemned homosexuality, and those who engaged in such acts were subject to death.

United States

In the United States, there has been a large problem of states assuming they can interfere with people's personal lives. We have already detailed how this interference has affected women and their choices with their bodies, but this interference has extended to sodomy laws that outlaw homosexual practices.

For example, in 1986, in a 5–4 decision in *Bowers v. Hardwick*, the U.S. Supreme Court upheld a Georgia sodomy law rejecting the right to privacy for gay adults, citing examples of the country's Judeo-Christian heritage and the believed proscriptions against homosexuality in the Bible in its reasoning.[83]

Forgetting the government cannot gratify religious intolerance and punish the private behaviors of the individuals, the U.S. Supreme Court didn't invalidate sodomy laws across the country until 2003 with its ruling in *Lawrence v. Texas* (yes, it took this long for anything to be done about the law). Justice Anthony Kennedy, who wrote the majority opinion, recognized the right to individual privacy, and that each person should be shielded by state intrusion into issues of morality. He saw what so many failed to see prior to this decision—that criminalizing the private conduct of people for one minor action, sodomy, would open the flood gates to imposing moral stances about sexuality through criminal law. That did not stop our beloved Justice Antonin Scalia from stating that this decision opened the door to "licentiousness . . . laws against bigamy, same-sex marriage, adult incest, prostitution, masturbation, adultery, fornication, bestiality, and obscenity"—all now permissible according to him.[84]

Justice Scalia does not seem to realize what people who identify as homosexual, transgender, or transsexual have faced over the centuries—nor, it seems, what they continue to face in the twenty-first century. As an example, Bill McCartney, founder of the men's rights activst group Promise Keepers, has called homosexuals "stark raving mad—[a] group of people who don't reproduce but want to be compared to people who do ... that lifestyle doesn't entitle anyone to special rights." Or consider James Dobson, founder of the anti-gay group Focus on the Family, who believes homosexuality is a disease, a threat to the (atomic) family, the health of the nation, and Christianity. He also likens marriage equality to bestiality. "It's a beast," he says. "It wants our kids ... How about marriage between a man and his donkey?"[85] Until a donkey can consent to marriage and sign a marriage certificate, Dobson has no argument.

Furthering the point, Bill Maier, vice president and psychologist for Focus on the Family, says gay marriage is "the most radical social experiment ever proposed ... [it is] redefining the institution of marriage." Melissa Fryrear, a so-called ex-lesbian, blames abusive parents on homosexuality. Robert H Knight, in his pamphlet distributed by Focus on the Family titled "The Homosexual Agenda in Schools," writes that homosexuality is "against God's ordained natural order, what they do is perverted and pathological." Peter LaBarbera, of the Illinois Family Institute (another anti-gay group), has called homosexuals "extremely promiscuous" and homoeroticism "gross, unnatural, dangerous behavior." He has even suggested physical violence against them, stating, "we've been too nice ... we need some people to do tough things."[86] And Pat Robertson, host of the *700 Club*, blames, among other things, gays and infidelity on the September 11, 2001 terrorist attacks.[87]

A pamphlet that circulated in the past decade, titled "Protect Your Family and Friends from the Dangers of Homosexuality: The Truth!" claimed "homosexuals carry the bulk of all bowel diseases in the USA" and "average

500 [sexual] partners in their short lifetime." Rod Parsley, head of the World Harvest Church, got Ohio voters to the polls in 2004 to help ban same-sex marriage in the state by questioning the biological basis for homosexuality. He stated that the lifestyle was physically and morally damaging and "liberals" were looking to destroy the moral fiber of the nation." This is the same man who had church members tithe 10 percent of their annual salary to him—and who tells them to burn their bills and give him money instead: "I want your money. I deserve it. The church deserves it." On top of all this are the unscientific peer-review journals and institutions that cite "evidence" for a "cure" to homosexuality.[88]

It should come as no surprise that, in 2012, the U.S. Surgeon General released a study which showed that church-going individuals who sought to deny their true sexuality or gender identity were two to three times more likely to attempt or commit suicide than those who made no such denial.[89] For example, Reverend Dr. Mel White, a clergyman who was active in the evangelical movement and ghostwrote several autobiographies for the likes of Jerry Falwell, Pat Robertson, and Billy Graham, struggled with his sexuality until adulthood. He also struggled with depression and guilt, both of which worsened when his brother died. When he sought help from a church psychotherapist, he was told that he was not cooperating with the spirit of God, which further escalated his negative emotions toward his sexuality and resulted in his contemplation of suicide.[90]

The push to ostracize those who identify as homosexual, transgender, or transsexual does nothing to stop the practice of, or identification with, these labels or lifestyles. In fact, with over 450 animal species exhibiting homosexual behavior or same-sex preferences,[91] such practices are anything but "unnatural." Indeed, if there is a great designer to the cosmos, he/she/it clearly designed homosexuality to be a natural part of life, contrary to what modern moralists state. For those who don't identify as LGBTQ, the research shows that, the best way to help LGBTQ individuals avoid depression, guilt, or any negative consequences, is to wholly accept the identity and romantic preferences of each individual.[92]

On the Bright Side

There is a lot of hostility toward the LGBTQ community within many Christian churches. But based on scripture itself, this hostility is clearly misplaced and need not be there. What is astounding is that the message coming from these churches shows either blatant ignorance or intentional avoidance of the positive messages related to homosexuality and gender nonconformity found within the Bible, particularly in the gospel accounts of Jesus' life and ministry.

One of the most common words in Greek, and a word never found in the gospels, is the one for romantic love, *eros*.[93] Surprisingly, there is only one passage in the New Testament that says Jesus "loved" any single individual—specifically, the story of Lazarus' resurrection (Gospel of John 11:3, 36) refers to the male disciple "Jesus loved" (13:23; 19:26; 20:2; 21:7). John 13 further states that Jesus' love for the "beloved disciple" was different from his love for the others. The word for "beloved" in Greek is *eromenos*, which is what Greek boys in pederastic relationships were called. Ergo, in the Gospel of John, it could be argued that the "beloved disciple" is actually a youthful apprentice to Jesus, in the same way boys were mentored in ancient Greek society in exchange for interfemoral intercourse.[94]

In Luke 7:1–10, we find a story of a centurion approaching Jesus. He tells Jesus that his "slave" is sick, to the point of death, and that this servant is highly valued to him. Jesus ends up healing the "slave" when he hears of the centurion's faith in him. I have chosen to put the word "slave" in quotations because, in the original text, that is not close to the word that the original Greek uses or implies. In Greek, the word for slave is *doulos*, but the word actually used in Luke is *pais*. This word, which means "boyfriend," was often used to imply a pederastic relationship. With this more precise language, this story clearly shows that Jesus does not condemn, nor turn away, someone in a homoerotic relationship.

In terms of gender identification, we learn some interesting things, again, about Jesus and the views held in antiquity about the matter—or, at least, how some views were reflected in the writings of the Bible. It is commonly known that Jesus, as well as Paul of Tarsus and John the Baptist, were ascetics—that is, they were people who gave up vices in life, like sex, alcohol, and money, to obtain a closer relationship with their God and to prepare for the end of the world. Such individuals, who would not marry or who felt marriage was not right for them, were called eunuchs, or *euriochoi* in Greek. But the word also refers to individuals who would not participate in sexual relationships. As Matthew 19:10–12 shows, "For there are eunuchs who have been so from birth, and there are eunuchs who have been made eunuchs by others, *and there are eunuchs who have made themselves eunuchs for the sake of the kingdom of heaven*. Let anyone accept this who can." Not only does this imply that Jesus was okay with eunuchs, whether they were a literal eunuch or simply an individual who refused sex or marriage like he did, but it also shows that, at the very least, the early church accepted people who were eunuchs.

By looking at texts like the Gospel of Thomas and Gospel of Mary Magdala, we get still another view of the meaning of the term. In those texts, eunuch suggested femininization, or a male preferring a female role. Jesus even tells the disciples, in saying 22 of the Gospel of Thomas, "when you make the male and the female one and the same, so that the male not be male and the female female . . . then will you enter the kingdom of heaven." This line refers to breaking out of the gender barriers set up by society and advocates gender nonconformity. We see similar ideas in the canonical gospels—for example, when Jesus tells the disciples in Luke 22:10 to look for a man carrying a water jug. In today's terms, that would be the equivalent of asking them to find a man wearing lipstick, as carrying water was considered a woman's job. And, it should be noted, so was washing people's feet, as Jesus did in John 13:1–20.[95] So, even though there is no explicit prescription for abolishing gender identity, Jesus' actions and words in the canonical gospels very subtly imply knowledge about and acceptance of gender nonconformity.

Conclusion

There is nothing from Jesus' mouth or actions that indicate he, or even the original authors of the New Testament, felt homosexuality, homoeroticism, transgenderism, or transsexuality were negative or worthy of punishment. What we see in our modern society are groups of people who do not understand the Bible's original message—or the importance of being able to participate in a relationship or lifestyle that aligns with one's personal sexual or gender identity. Indeed, based on the actions carried out against LGTBQ individuals within recent memory, they face far more barbarism today than they did in Jesus' day. To be quite blunt, modern evangelical Christian "moralists" preach a very anti-Christian message. They are not moralists, and they do not proselytize with a message of love, or even promote Jesus' message. They are people full of vitriol and hate who selectively choose passages that fit their own discomfort and give credence to their own phobias and dislike of other people's life choices. If Jesus did preach a ministry of inclusion, gender nonconformity, and, most of all, love, then he certainly wouldn't approve of groups like the Westboro Baptist Church, which stand on street corners and at funerals holding signs that read "God Hates Fags," let alone individuals who beat, torture, or murder people for being gay or transgender. Let us call such groups and individuals for what they are: vile bigots.

Notes

1. As cited in "Gays and Lesbians," Leadership Conference on Civil and Human Rights, www.civilrights.org/resources/civilrights101/sexualorientation.html (accessed August 8, 2014).

2. As cited in Amanda Terkel, "LGBT Applicants Less Likely to Be Called Back for Interviews with Federal Contractors, Study Shows," *Huffington Post*, June 30, 2014, http://m.huffpost.com/us/entry/5538195.

3. "Gay and Bisexual Men's Health: Stigma and Discrimination," Center for Disease Control and Prevention, updated March 3, 2011 www.cdc.gov/msmhealth/stigma-and-discrimination.htm (accessed August 8, 2014).

4. James Brooke, "Witnesses Trace Brutal Killing of Gay Student," *New York Times*, August 21, 1998, www.nytimes.com/1998/11/21/us/witnesses-trace-brutal-killing-of-gay-student.html.

5. Philip L. DuBois, Matthew Shepard Resource Site, www.uwyo.edu/news/shepard.

6. Nicole Hensley, "Seattle Fugitive Suspected of Killing Two Gay Men Nabbed in New Jersey," *Daily News*, July 19, 2014, http://tinyurl.com/lw878we.

7. Sasha Goldstein, "Texas Dad Killed Daughter, Her Lesbian Lover Because He Disliked That She Was Gay: Mom," *Daily News*, March 14, 2014, http://tinyurl.com/mfd9xan.

8. Miranda Leitsinger, "Authorities Arrest Man Who Allegedly Shot Lesbian Teen Couple in Texas," *NBC News*, June 21, 2014, http://tinyurl.com/ps49798.

9. Nick Duffy, "South Africa: Teens Watch as Gay Man Is Beaten, Murdered and Set on Fire," *Pink News*, March 28, 2014, http://tinyurl.com/ngosplj.

10. "Wife and Mother Was Brutally Stabbed to Death by Her Husband of 19 Years after He Learned of Her Lesbian Fling with a Younger Woman," *Daily Mail Online*, revised May 2, 2014, http://tinyurl.com/qh65k3l.

11. Rebecca Cathcart, "Boys Killing Labeled a Hate Crime, Stuns a Town," *New York Times*, February 23, 2008, http://www.nytimes.com/2008/02/23/us/23oxnard.html?_r=0.

12. "Police: Murder Victim Convinced Suspect He Was a Girl," *RTV6 Indianapolis*, August 1, 2003, http://tinyurl.com/oygm7p7.

13. Jim Spellman, "Transgender Murder, Hate Crime,

Conviction a First", *CNN*, April 23, 2009, http://tinyurl.com/cq2a5c.

14. Nissinen, *Homoeroticism*, 39.

15. John Boswell, *Christianity, Social Tolerance, and Homosexuality* (Chicago: Chicago University Press, 1980), 100.

16. Nissinen, *Homoeroticism*, 46.

17. Friedman and Dolansky, *The Bible Now*, 5.

18. Friedman and Dolansky, *The Bible Now*, 8.

19. Eugene Volokh, "What Percentage of the U.S. Population Is Gay, Lesbian, or Bisexual?" *Washington Post*, July 15, 2014, https://www.washingtonpost.com/news/volokh-conspiracy/wp/2014/07/15/what-percentage-of-the-u-s-population-is-gay-lesbian-or-bisexual/.

20. Friedman and Dolansky, *The Bible Now*, 34.

21. Nissinen, *Homoeroticism*, 48.

22. Nissinen, *Homoeroticism*, 43.

23. Friedman and Dolansky, *The Bible Now*, 19–20.

24. Nissinen, *Homoeroticism*, 105–7.

25. Nissinen, *Homoeroticism,* 113–17.

26. Boswell, *Christianity*, 106–7.

27. Coogan, *God and Sex*, 95.

28. Coogan, *God and Sex*, 96.

29. Friedman and Dolansky, *The Bible Now*, 27.

30. Nissinen, *Homoeroticism*, 19–20.

31. Nissinen, *Homoeroticism*, 23–24.

32. Nissinen, *Homoeroticism,* 25–27.

33. Nissinen, *Homoeroticism*, 57–59.

34. Boswell, *Christianity*, 92.

35. Nissinen, *Homoeroticism*, 66, 68.

36. Friedman and Dolansky, *The Bible Now*, 28.

37. Boswell, *Christianity*, 61.

38. Nissinen, *Homoeroticism*, 70.

39. Nissinen, *Homoeroticism*, 73.

40. Felix Minucius and Rendall Marcus, *Octavius*, ed. H. Gerald and W. C. A. Kerr (Cambridge: Harvard University Press, 1931).

41. Nissinen, *Homoeroticism*, 70.

42. Boswell, *Christianity,* 69.

43. Boswell, *Christianity*, 65.

44. Nissinen, *Homoeroticism*, 70.

45. Boswell, *Christianity*, 74–78.

46. Boswell, *Christianity*, 82.

47. Nissinen, *Homoeroticism*, 36.

48. Nissinen, *Homoeroticism*, 75.

49. Nissinen, *Homoeroticism*, 77.

50. Nissinen, *Homoeroticism*.

51. Boswell, *Christianity*, 82.

52. The original reads, *"non fellat (putat hoc parum virile), sed plane medias vorat puellas. di mentem tibi dent tuam, Philaeni, cunnum lingere wuae putas virile."* Martial, "Epigram LXVII, Book VII," as cited in *The Lesbian Pillow Book*, ed. Alison Hennegan (London: Fourth Estate, 2000).

53. Nissinen, *Homoeroticism*, 30–31, 33.

54. Nissinen, *Homoeroticism*.

55. Juvenal, *Satire 6*, ed. Lindsay Watson and Patricia Watson, (New York: Cambridge University Press, 2014), 186.

56. Boswell, *Christianity*, 76.

57. Boswell, *Christianity*, 104.

58. Richard J. Bauckham, "The Letter of Jude," in *The Harper Collins Study Bible* (New York: HarperCollins Publishers, 2006), 2085.

59. "Saul of Tarsus (known as Paul, the Apostle of the Heathen)," in *The Jewish Encyclopedia* (1906, 2011), http://www.jewishencyclopedia.com/articles/11952-paul-of-tarsus.

60. Armstrong, *Myth*, 43–44.

61. Boswell, *Christianity*, 99.

62. Josephus, *Antiquities of the Jews,* trans. William Whiston (Massachusetts: Tufts University Press, 1895).

63. Thomas A. J. McGinn, *Prostitution, Sexuality, and the Law in Ancient Rome* (New York: Oxford University Press, 2003), 159.

64. Nissinen, *Homoeroticism*, 95.

65. Boswell, *Christianity*, 148.

66. Cornelius Tacitus, *The Annals*, ed. Alfred John Churchman and William Jackson Brodribb (New York: Random House, Inc., 1942).

67. Willaim Stearns Davis, ed., *Readings in Ancient History: Illustrative Extracts from the Sources, Vol. 2: Rome and the West* (Massachusetts: Allyn and Bacon, 1913), 196–210, 215–22, 250–51, 289–90, 295–96, 298–300.

68. Boswell, *Christianity*, 132.

69. Boswell, *Christianity*, 139.

70. Theresa Tinkle, *Medieval Venuses and Cupids: Sexuality, Hermeneutics, and English Poetry* (Redwood City: Stanford University Press, 1996), 83.

71. Boswell, *Christianity*, 141–42.

72. Boswell, *Christianity*, 149–51, 161.

73. Boswell, *Christianity*, 79, 121–22.

74. Louis Crompton, *Homosexuality and Civilization* (Cambridge: Harvard University Press, 2009), 145.

75. Boswell, *Christianity*, 173–74.

76. Cristian Berco, "Spain," in *glbtq*, http://www.glbtq.com/social-sciences/spain.html (accessed October 15, 2014).

77. David F. Greenberg, *The Construction of Homosexuality* (Illinois: University of Chicago Press, 1990), 288.

78. Boswell, *Christianity*, 280–83.

79. Boswell, *Christianity*, 271.

80. Gary Taylor, *Castration: An Abrreviated History of Western Manhood* (Florence: Psychology Press, 2002), 283.

81. Boswell, *Christianity*, 290.

82. Thomas Aquinas, *Summa Theologica, Part II–II (Secunda Secundae)*, trans. Fathers of the English Dominican Province (Christian Classics Ethereal Library, 2014), www.ccel.org.

83. Sehat, *Myth*, 273–74.

84. Sehat, *Myth*, 279–80.

85. Hedges, *Fascists*, 92, 98–99, 106.

86. Hedges, *Fascists*, 115.

87. Hedges, *Fascists*, 106–9.

88. Hedges, *Fascists*, 122, 137–38, 161, 166.

89. Office of the Surgeon General and National Action Alliance for Suicide Prevention, *National Strategy for Suicide Prevention Goals and Objectives for Action* (Washington, DC: U.S. Department of National Health and Human Services , September 2012), 121–22.

90. Hedges, *Fascists*, 110–13.

91. Arash Fereydoonim, "Do Animals Exhibit Homosexuality?" *Yale Scientific Magazine*, March 14, 2012, http://www.yalescientific.org/2012/03/do-animals-exhibit-homosexuality/.

92. Kristofor Husted, "Family Acceptance Key in Preventing Gay Youths From Considering Suicide," *NPR*, February 14, 2012, http://tinyurl.com/meds2lm.

93. Bernard V. Brady, *Christian Love* (Washington, DC: Georgetown University Press, 2003), 53.

94. Theodore W. Jennings, Jr., *The Man Jesus Loved* (Cleveland: Pilgrim Press, 2009), 14, 22.

95. Jennings, *Loved*, 160, 163–65.

5

Circumcision

In October 2010, a woman in Oregon was arrested and tried for assault. Not for physical violence against another full-grown adult, but for attempting to circumcise her three-month-old son herself. She divulged that she had used a box cutter and pliers, the latter as a tourniquet, to perform the surgery. It was carried out in front of her thirteen-year-old son, who became extremely upset, particularly when the procedure did not go well. After a failed attempt to sew up the wound, the child bled for two hours before the mother called paramedics. She had attempted it herself because the local hospitals would not perform the procedure on children older than four weeks. So what caused her to suddenly want to cut off her son's foreskin? What made her suddenly decide to carry out such a barbaric deed, with her medical knowledge about the procedure based only on a YouTube video? Simple: she stated she was moved to do so because she had read the Bible.[1]

After the incident, she spent twenty-eight days in jail and underwent psychiatric treatment. Sentenced to time spent and five years of probation, she is no longer able to see her children without supervision.[2] I do not include this story here to suggest religion is a mental health issue. That is not my place to determine, though the woman's attorney did indicate that the action was "an aberation during a down period in her life." While I cannot guess what her personal life or mental health was like at the time of the incident, it might be fair to say she was struggling pretty badly in order to feel it okay, even necessary, to commit such an action. According to Kenneth I. Pargament, PhD, "religion and spirituality are generally helpful to people in coping, especially people with the fewest resources facing the most uncontrollable problems."[3]

Child safety is the major concern in such circumstances. In October 2013, a woman filed suit against a pediatric healthcare clinic for cutting "too much" and damaging her son's genitals. He was eventually, after an examination by another doctor, taken to a urologist, where he was properly treated.[4] In April 2013, two mohels, the individuals responsible for performing circumcisions on infants according to Jewish tradition, were banned from performing the ultra-Orthodox practice called *metzitzah b'peh*, which entails the mohel placing his mouth over the penis once the foreskin is removed and sucking out a small portion of blood. The reason they were banned? Herpes transmission. Since 2000, thirteen infants have contracted herpes in New York City due to this practice; with two children dying from the disease.[5]

Let us not ignore the issue of female circumcision—often referred to as female genital mutilation. In September 2014, a man was arrested after his family stepped forward and told police that he had removed a woman's clitoris with a razor blade "for his own direct sexual gratification." The family was from the Ivory Coast, a country where, among many others in Africa, female circumcision is regularly performed as a way to "control a woman's sexuality."[6] The procedure, unlike the one performed on males, is not advocated for by any medical association. An estimated three million women are subjected to the practice each year worldwide, including within certain immigrant communities in the United States.[7]

What Does the Bible Say?

Circumcision, with regard to the Abrahamic faiths, allegedly goes back to Abraham and his covenant with God. Genesis 17:10 states, "This is my covenant, which you shall keep, between me and you and your offspring after you: Every male among you shall be circumcised." (In essence, God disliked that one thing about his "perfect creation" so much that he demanded it be surgically removed.) For those who refused, Genesis 17:14 states, "Any uncircumcised male who is not circumcised in the flesh of his foreskin shall be cut off from his people; he has broken my covenant." I suspect that this procedure was meant to distinguish the people of Israel from their neighboring communities. Though some groups, like the Egyptian tribes who lived in Canaan prior to the Israelites, did practice circumcision, it may have arisen in part as a distinguishing feature to separate the Israelites from others.[8] It certainly was a clear ethnic marker during the

Israelite's exile in Babylon in the sixth century BCE, when portions of the Pentateuch, or the five books of Moses, were written, including Genesis.[9]

The Hebrew word for circumcision is *milah,* or *berit milah,* meaning "covenant of circumcision." In Judaism, it entails cutting away the foreskin eight days after the birth of the child, even if that day falls on the Sabbath or Yom Kippur (the Day of Atonement). Circumcision is postponed only if the procedure is viewed as being detrimental to the child's health. Traditionally, being uncircumcised meant you were excluded from important Jewish rites and rituals, and it has thus been an important sign of being a Jew. Though Jewish Hellenists attempted to get rid of the practice, bringing in Greco-Roman ideologies into the faith, the practice has remained an integral rite within Judaism across the centuries, even among otherwise nonobservant Jews.[10]

As discussed, there is a fascinating story in Exodus 4:24–26 that involves circumcision as well. In this story, God attacks Moses. In response, Moses' wife, Zipporah, quickly grabs a flint, circumcises their son (ouch!), and holds the foreskin to Moses' "feet" (i.e., his genitals). Very pleased, God leaves them be. What can we determine from this story? First, Moses may not have been circumcised; and second, circumcision, aside from being a rite of passage into the faith, may also have been practiced as a ritual marking marriage or puberty.[11]

Joshua 5:2–9 furthers the idea that circumcision should be performed as a religious practice and that religious rituals can be practiced *only* by those who have gone through the initiation of circumcision. Here, God commands Joshua to circumcise those who had survived the desert pilgrimage from Egypt to the holy land of Israel. He had the people wait until they were in Canaan, the land that was Israel before the Israelites' inhabitation of it. Only after they were circumcised could they then celebrate the Passover, as seen in Joshua 5:10. A similar idea is shared in Exodus 12:48: "A foreigner residing among you who wants to celebrate the LORD's Passover must have all the males in his household circumcised; then he may take part like one born in the land. No uncircumcised male may eat it."

Circumcision is also used in a metaphorical sense. We see this in Jeremiah 6:10: "To whom shall I give warning, that they may hear? See, their ears are uncircumcised, they cannot listen." What did it mean to have an uncircumcised ear? It meant that the people Jeremiah was speaking of would not accept the teachings from Yahweh, and it was as if their ears would not open to, what the Israelites viewed as, the divine truth. Ergo, their ears were uncircumcised. Similarly, to have an uncircumcised heart meant to be stubborn. We see this in Leviticus 26:41 and Jeremiah 9:25–26.[12]

In the New Testament, the debate over circumcision takes a drastic turn away from the teachings of the Hebrew Bible thanks to Paul of Tarsus. In Acts 15:1, we get insight into the actions that led to the Council of Jerusalem, which would eventually determine Christians need not observe most Mosaic laws: "certain individuals came down from Judea and were teaching the brothers, 'Unless you are circumcised according to the customs of Moses, you cannot be saved.'" In Galatians 2:11–14, we see how upset Paul was about this idea: "When Peter came to Antioch, I opposed him to his face because he was clearly in the wrong . . . I said to Peter in front of all of them, 'You are a Jew, yet you live like a Gentile and not a Jew. How is it, then, that you force Gentiles to follow Jewish customs?'" Although it is clear from Paul's letters that the original sect that was closest to Jesus felt circumcision was necessary, particularly for converts from the Gentile world, Paul himself was clearly anti-circumcision. He saw it as part of the old covenant that Jesus, as Christ, now superseded. At Galatians 6:15, he writes, "For in Christ Jesus neither circumcision availeth any thing, nor uncircumcision, but a new creature."[13]

So why was circumcision suddenly off the table for Paul? Why was it such a huge issue, especially when confronted by Peter and the Jerusalem Council, which included John and James, Jesus' brother? Writes Alan F. Segal, "For Paul, the critical issue for faith was to be in Christ. For people of the spirit, the flesh was secondary." In this regard, Paul did not believe Gentile converts needed to be circumcised, especially given the one-and-done nature of circumcision. Paul was equally if not more concerned with doing away with dietary restrictions—in large part due to the very public nature of food-related rituals.[14] Thus, while Paul advocated for a release from circumcision and dietary law, those closest to Jesus held a different position.[15] For example, in Galatians 2:11–14, Peter refuses to eat with the Gentiles.

Paul's beliefs are so unmovable that, even when his companion Titus tells him he wants to be circumcised, Paul rebukes him. This is a sharp contrast to what Acts 16 says about Paul's views on circumcision. Paul actually has another follower, Timothy, undergo circumcision in order to appease the Jews. But elsewhere, in Galatians 1:6–7, Paul voice's his disappointment that people doubt what Jesus revealed to him in his visions.[16] Paul is also vocal against "the circumcisers" in Galatians 2:12, "for until certain people came from James, he used to eat with the Gentiles. But after they came, he drew back and kept himself separate for fear of the circumcision faction." Further, Paul felt that adherence to circumcision meant making oneself a slave to Jewish law. In Galatians 5:1–4, he warns, "do not submit again to a yoke of slavery . . . if you let yourself be circumcised, Christ will be of no benefit to you. Once again I testify to every man who lets himself be circumcised that he is obliged to obey the entire law."

The bigger struggle between the Jerusalem Council and Paul was overadherence to Jewish law. It became so heated that, eventually, the name of Jesus' brother, James, becomes interchangeable in Paul's letters with the word "law," which Paul views as obsolete thanks to Jesus' intervention.[17] Paul was more concerned about people being a Jew inwardly rather than outwardly. Someone could be circumcised, but this would not necessarily mean they accepted Jesus as Christ. This view is part of the reason Paul was sexually abstinent and advocated for others to be so (Galatians 5:16). He felt if those who followed Christ could change their feelings and behavior internally, then externally it should not matter if they were circumcised or followed dietary law.[18] It is thanks, in part, to Paul that, by the end of the first century, the majority of Christian groups consisted of Gentiles in Greece, Asia Minor, Italy, and Egypt. And each Gentile-Christian group claimed that *they* were the true embodiment of Israel.[19]

Because of Paul's persuasiveness, baptism replaced circumcision as the new covenant, instilled through Jesus as Christ. Accordingly, Colossians 2:11–12 reads, "In him you were circumcised with a spiritual circumcision ["a circumcision without hands" in the original Greek] . . . when you were buried with him in baptism, you were also raised with him through faith in the power of God, who raised him from the dead." Thus, baptism went from being a ritual that recreated the rising up out of the Red Sea, with the Israelites escaping from Egypt, to an act that represented Jesus being buried and raised from the dead. Even though some individuals continued to look to circumcision as a way to further their initiation into the cult that was the Jesus movement in Judaism, Paul advocated for knowledge. He felt that true initiation happened through one's growth in knowledge and moral behaviors, which would provide a divine *dynamis*, or ability. After all, with the (assumed) end of the world coming, who would want to undergo painful circumcision when baptism would be sufficient?[20]

Outside of the Bible

Circumcision is generally regarded as one of the world's oldest surgical practices. Some date it as beginning as far back as 15,000 years ago. It's believed to have been used as a way to mark captured slaves as an alternative to castration, a practice that carried with it a much greater risk of death. The earliest evidence we have of circumcision is an image of an adult being circumcised found in the Egyptian tomb of Ankh-Mahor, which dates to 2400–2300 BCE. In this case, the procedure was believed to have been done for hygiene, as a way to keep sand from getting under the foreskin and from irritating the glans (head) of the penis. It may also have been a rite of passage from childhood to adulthood.[21] Later cultures in the region also likely practiced circumcision, such as the Sumerians, Phoenicians, and Babylonians.[22]

Antiochus Epiphanes, a Hellenistic king of the Seleucid Empire in the second century BCE, was clearly not a fan of Jews. We know this from the account in 1 Maccabees, where he is shown to outlaw not just circumcision but also Torah study and Sabbath observance. These acts, in large part, led to the Maccabean, or Jewish, revolt against him.[23] The Greeks were repulsed by circumcision, viewing it as genital mutilation. We also know that, prior to the revolt, in order to not upset Epiphanes, some Jews had operations to disguise their circumcision, which created an uproar within Jewish communities.[24]

Toward the end of the first century BCE and into the beginning of the first century CE, Philo of Alexandria, a Hellenized Jew, viewed people who practiced circumcision as "extreme allegorists." He felt, as many Hellenized Jews did, that circumcision, as well as dietary restrictions, were metaphorical and did not need to be practiced literally.[25] Even Plutarch (45–120 CE), another Alexandrian Jew, rejected the literalism in the Torah and abandoned the practice of circumcision and dietary laws.[26] In addition, the Gospel of Thomas, a gnostic text dating somewhere between 50 and 100 CE that consists of 114 sayings of Jesus, reads, at saying 53, "If [circumcision] were useful, their father would produce children already circumcised."[27] These passages suggest that, even in the earliest days of the Jesus movement of Judaism, circumcision was already questioned and seen as unnecessary by some.

In 1442, with the 11th Council of Florence, the Church came to expressly favor baptism over circumcision, much in the same way Paul of Tarsus did. In fact, the council goes so far as to state, "[The Catholic Church] denounces all who ... observe circumcision, the [Jewish] sabbath, and other legal prescriptions as strangers to the faith of Christ and unable to share in eternal salvation, unless they recoil at some time from these errors."[28]

After this, much of the discussion about circumcision related to its supposed medical merits. In 1870, for example, Dr. Lewis Sayre, founder of the American Medical Association, claimed that circumcision could cure paralysis or motor skill problems in young boys. This claim stemmed from, what was known as, the reflex neurosis theory—specifically, that excessive stimulation of the genitals caused a disturbance in a boy's equilibrium.[29] Because of this belief, doctors also thought circumcision could cure epilepsy, impotence, and insanity.[30] Elsewhere, a British doctor found that Jews had a lower prevalence of venereal disease than other groups and thus advocated for the practice of circumcision, work which earned him a knighthood.[31] Even well into the twentieth century, the foreskin was believed to cause infection by catching and collecting smegma, a mixture of shed skin cells and body oils, which made circumcision an almost universally recommended procedure with male births in the United States.[32]

In more recent years, new medical evidence has helped moderate the perceived need for the procedure. During a period of roughly three decades, from 1979 to 2010, the rate of newborn circumcision dropped from 64.9 to 58.3 percent in the United States. The highest rate was in 1981, at 64.9 percent, and the lowest was in 2007, at 55.4 percent. This drop in rates of newborn circumcision came largely from the changing perspective of the medical community. In 1989, for example, the American Association of Pediatrics claimed there were potential benefits to having children circumcised, but, in 1999, the very same group said the evidence was insufficient to support the necessity of circumcision, let alone to conclude that there are any benefits to the procedure.[33]

Conclusion

Circumcision remains an extremely common practice in the United States, despite the trend away from it and mounting medical evidence against it.[34] In the case of Judaism, the covenant is clear. However, those Christians who advocate for circumcision on religious grounds, such as the Oregon woman who mutilated her three-month-old son's genitals, do so based only on Genesis in the Old Testament and not on the writings of Paul in the New Testament. The result? Each year millions of infants have their genitals mutilated for little more than their parents' belief that they are fulfilling a command from the Abrahamic God.[35]

Notes

1. Paul Thompson, "Oregon Woman 'Used Box Cutters and Pliers to Circumcise Three-Month-Old Son at Home … after Learning How on YouTube,'" *Daily Mail*, April 12, 2011, http://www.dailymail.co.uk/news/article-1375793/Oregon-woman-used-box-cutter-pliers-circumcise-son-home.html.

2. Helen Jung, "Portland Woman Who Botched Circumcision of 3-Month-Old Son Gets Probation, Ordered to Undergo Mental Health Treatment," *Oregonian*, August 15, 2011, http://www.oregonlive.com/portland/index.ssf/2011/08/portland_woman_who_botched_cir.html.

3. "What Role Do Religion and Spirituality Play in Mental Health?" American Psychological Association, March 22, 2013, http://www.apa.org/news/press/releases/2013/03/religion-spirituality.aspx.

4. "Mom Sues Pediatrics Center, Says Son's Genitals Damaged during Circumcision," *Fox8 News*, October 1, 2014, http://myfox8.com/2014/10/01/mom-sues-pediatrics-center-says-sons-genitals-damaged-during-circumcision/.

5. Brittany Brady, "Babies' Herpes Linked to Circumcision Practice," *CNN*, April 8, 2013, http://www.cnn.com/2013/04/07/health/new-york-neonatal-herpes/.

6. Rocco Parascandola, Shayna Jacobs, Joseph Stepansky, and Bill Hutchinson, "African Immigrant Accused of Performing Female Circumcision with Razor Blade," *New York Daily News*, October 7, 2014, http://tinyurl.com/k5vav5k.

7. "Education," Safe Hands for Safe Girls, http://www.safehandsforgirls.org/education.html (accessed October 22, 2014).

8. A. Totaro et al., A. Volpe, M. Racioppi, F. Pinto, E. Sacco, P. F. Bassi, "Circumcision: History, Religion and Law," *Urologia* 78, no. 1 (January–March 2011): 1–9, http://www.ncbi.nlm.nih.gov/pubmed/21452153.

9. Mordecai Cogan, "Into Exile: From the Assyrian Conquest of Israel to the Fall of Babylon," in *The Oxford History of the Biblical World* (New York: Oxford University Press, 1998), 271.

10. Geoffrey Wigoder, ed., "Circumcision," in *The Standard Jewish Encyclopedia*, 7th ed. (New York: Facts on File, Inc., 1992), 216.

11.   Glenn S. Holland, *Gods in the Desert: Religions of the Ancient Near East* (Lanham: Rowman and Littlefield Publishers, 2009), 263.

12.   George Wesley Buchanan, "Circumcision," in *The Oxford Guide to the Bible* (New York: Oxford University Press, 1993), 123–24.

13.   Buchanan, "Circumcision."

14.   Alan F. Segal, *Paul the Convert* (New Haven: Yale University Press, 1990), 224.

15.   E. P. Sanders, *The Historical Figure of Jesus* (New York: Penguin Publishers, 1993), 221–22.

16.   Bart D. Ehrman, *Peter, Paul, and Mary Magdalene* (New York: Oxford University Press, 2006), 99, 125, 155.

17.   Robert Eisenman, *James: The Brother of Jesus* (New York: Penguin Books, 1998), 129–31.

18.   Pagels, *Serpent*, 8.

19.   Elaine Pagels, *The Origin of Satan* (New York: Vintage Books, 1995), 63.

20.   Luke Timothy Johnson, *Among the Gentiles* (New Haven: Yale University Press, 2009), 139, 146, 162–63.

21.   David Gollaher, *Circumcision: A History of the World's Most Controversial Surgery* (New York: Basic Books, 2001), 1–30.

22.   D. Doyle, "Ritual Male Circumcision: A Brief History," *Journal of the Royal College of Physicians of Edinburgh* 35, no. 3 (2005): 279–85, http://www.rcpe.ac.uk/publications/articles/journal_35_3/doyle_circumcision.pdf.

23.   Pagels, *Satan*, 45.

24.   Sanders, *Jesus*, 16–17.

25.   Amy-Jill Levine, "Visions of Kingdoms: From Pompey to the First Jewish Revolt," in *The Oxford Guide to the Biblical World* (New York: Oxford University Press, 1998), 376.

26. Johnson, *Gentiles*, 116.

27. Robert E. Van Voorst, *Jesus Outside the New Testament: An Introduction to the Ancient Evidence* (Grand Rapids: Wm. B. Eerdmans Publishing, 2000), 189.

28. Norman P. Tanner, ed., "Ecumenical Council of Florence (1438–1445): Session 11–4 February 1442; Bull of Union with the Copts," *Decree of the Ecumenical Councils,* 2nd ed. (Washington DC: Georgetown University Press, 1990).

29. Robert Darby, *A Surgical Temptation: The Demonization of the Foreskin and the Rise of Circumcision in Britain* (Chicago: University of Chicago Press, 2005), 262.

30. Vern L. and Bonnie Bullough, *Human Sexuality: An Encyclopedia* (New York: Garland Press, 1994), 426.

31. Darby, *Temptation*, 262.

32. Gollaher, *Circumcision*, 73–108.

33. Rachael Rettner, "U.S. Circumcision Rate Drops over Last 3 Decades, Report Says," *Huffington Post*, August 22, 2013, updated April 7, 2014, www.huffingtonpost.com/2014/04/07/circumcision-rate-drops_n_5107637.html.

34. J. M. Hutson, "Circumcision: A Surgeon's Perspective," *Journal of Medical Ethics* 30 (2004): 238–40, http://www.jme.bmj.com/content/30/3/238.full.

35. Leonard B. Glick, *Marked in Your Flesh: Circumcision from Ancient Judea to Modern America* (New York: Oxford University Press, 2005), 7, 10.

6

Birth Control

In 2012, Sandra Fluke, a Georgetown law student, testified before Congress on behalf of a classmate who needed her birth control covered by her health insurance to manage and control her ovarian cysts, something the birth control pill is utilized for, aside from preventing pregnancy. Rush Limbaugh opted to jump on the airwaves and insist that Fluke, not the woman she was arguing on behalf of, was demanding that Congress pay for her to be "a slut, right? It makes her a prostitute . . . she's having so much sex she can't afford the contraception." He then made more crude comments about how women, specifically "feminazis," needed to return the favor of having their birth control covered by posting videos online of them having intercourse.[1] Such comments are par for the course for Limbaugh. During a July 2014 broadcast in which he lamented how the Affordable Care Act requires coverage for contraception, he stated, "In the normal, everyday flow of events, pregnancy requires action that has consequences. And yet we treat it as a great imposition that women need to be protected from; it's a sickness, it's a disease, it's whatever, and there's got to be a pill for it. And yet they wouldn't have a problem if they didn't do a certain thing. It's that simple."[2]

What we witness in Limbaugh's comments about birth control, among many other such comments by moralizing commentators and politicians, is a lack of education about the various reasons why the pill might be taken and a lack of understanding about how a woman's body works. More than that, we see an expression of a patriarchal society that assumes men can dictate the health care choices of the opposite gender. After all, we do not hear the same types of arguments against condoms.

What Does the Bible Say?

As with abortion, there are no biblical passages that directly prohibit birth control. This does not mean, however, that the concept of birth control was nonexistent in the Bible. Rather, the issue of birth control was never an intended focus in biblical stories. Consider, for example, the story of Onan in Genesis 38. As a brief recap, Onan's brother, Er, was killed because he "was wicked in the sight of the LORD." Because Er had no children, particularly male children, the levirate marriage custom dictated that Onan must marry Er's widow and provide a male descendent, who would be considered Er's child, not Onan's. But Onan had other plans: "since Onan knew that the offspring would not be his, he spilled his semen on the ground whenever he went in to his brother's wife, so that he would not give offspring to his brother." God in turn teaches Onan a lesson: "What he did was displeasing in the sight of the LORD, and he put him to death also." This story does not emphasize or pinpoint an error of birth control, nor does it even find error with the woman, but it does find error with the man, Onan. In short, God punished Onan because he refused to fulfill the levirate marriage custom, which had significance for a family's standing and lineage. Birth control is, very clearly, not a concern of God in this story.

The concept of the levirate marriage is further addressed in Deuteronomy 25:7–10. If a deceased husband's brother refuses to take the widowed woman, she has to approach "the elders," who then call the brother before them. If he still refuses, she is permitted to remove his sandal and spit in his face, which puts the title of any property he inherited through the woman to her own name. This ceremony was meant to publicly shame the brother and his family ("This is what is done to the man who does not build up his brother's house"), as their inaction would bring public shame to the woman, who would legally be called a "widow" and placed in a class of impoverished people, as seen in Deuteronomy 14:29: "the resident aliens, the orphans, and the widows."[3]

Genesis 4:1, sometimes cited in arguments against birth control, tells of the birth of Cain, whose name comes from the Hebrew *qanah*, meaning "to create."[4] In the story, Eve says, "I have produced a man with the help of the LORD." Similarly, at Genesis 33:5, when Esau sees the women and children with Jacob, he asks who they are, and Jacob replies, "The children whom God has graciously given your servant." Although God has indeed "gifted" children to them, it is important to note that these are individual accounts. These stories say nothing about every child being a gift, nor do they take into account individual choice—that is, whether the women chose to have children or were coerced or even forced into pregnancy.

More than that, the story of Cain reads like an etiology of the Kenite tribe known by ancient Israelites.[5] Like many other stories about the names of people and places, this story told about the origins of groups and areas and their relationships to nature. For example, consider how Jacob is renamed "Israel" in Genesis 32:28. The name, in its earliest phase, likely meant "El rules," with El being the Semitic god of the northwest pantheon. This account also provides a name, Peniel ("Face of God"), for the place where Jacob wrestled with God, as it was believed humanity could not see the face of God, but Jacob, who became Israel, did. Lastly, this same story also explains why Israelites are not permitted to eat thigh muscle, as that is where Jacob is struck during the altercation with God.[6] In other words, the Cain story had the purpose of telling about the origins of the Kenite tribe and had nothing to do with birth control.

At Genesis 33:5 Jacob offers up his family as slaves to Esau, who came to attack Jacob and his family, only to find Jacob, his wives, concubines, and children all ready to surrender. Another important point to make, therefore, is that this was not a story of how blessed Jacob was to have children, but one of him offering up his entire camp for slavery for betraying Esau and "stealing" the birthright given to him by their blind father. When Esau asks about them, Jacob says that he has brought them forward, "To find favor with my lord." Esau responds, "I have enough, my brother; keep what you have for yourself." In short, Jacob was sweet talking his brother in order to find favor and be kept from whatever punishment he imagined would come. He was not making an argument about being "blessed" with children.

Psalm 127:5 offers another passage used to show that God provides children as gifts, or heritage—more specifically, it should come as no surprise, the gift of *sons*. "Like arrows in the hand of a warrior are the sons of one's youth," says Psalm 127:4. But this passage is not about the "gift" of children, as people would understand the word today, but rather about the ability of men—sons—to protect a house, a family, and a community.[7] The passage is too specific in terms of gender and too concerned with the community as a whole to be interpreted as children being literal gifts from a deity.

In the New Testament, at Luke 1:42, a pregnant Mary goes to the house of the elderly Zechariah and Elizabeth. At the sound of Mary's voice, Elizabeth is filled with the Holy Spirit, declaring, "Blessed are you, and blessed is the fruit of your womb." As exciting and happy as this story is, Elizabeth's words refer only to Mary and the baby she was carrying, the Son of God. Elizabeth's declaration does not mean that *all* children are holy, nor is she giving a command or statement from God. This is a woman celebrating another woman's pregnancy, and it is one the author hopes to have declared as joyous. After all, would the author want to have a woman telling the mother of the coming Messiah that she should rethink her decision, or that she was not ready? Regardless of the ethics and modern-day morality we may want to project onto the story, the author wanted to portray a wonderful moment related to one woman and the coming birth of Jesus.

Nothing in these passages, when keeping their context in mind, suggests that every child is a gift, let alone a gift from God. There are no commands or statements from God in the Bible that would suggest he intended every pregnancy to be viewed as a gift from him. Nor is there any instance in the Bible of God stating that intercourse must result in pregnancy. Even if such a statement existed, the context of the time in which it was made would matter. As has already been stated, at the time the Bible was written each woman needed to have five children just to maintain the population.[8] With advances in medicine and science, the same is not true today. At present, the replacement fertility rate is just over two births per woman.[9] Thus, any biblical statement about birth control would not reflect our current circumstances and where we have come as a species.

Before the Bible

Contraception was not something foreign or unknown to biblical authors. The earliest documentation of contraception we have dates to about 600 years before the Israelite people. The Kahun Papyrus mentions contraception multiple times, or at least prescriptions believed to help prevent pregnancy. This included placing honey, acacia leaves, and lint (not necessarily all together) at the back of the vagina prior to intercourse.[10] It was also believed in ancient Egypt that breastfeeding, or lactation, could prevent pregnancy for up to three years.[11]

During the seventh century BCE, ancient Greeks used a plant called siliphium for its contraceptive abilities. The plant grew only on a small plot of land off the coast of Cyrene, or what is modern-day Libya. Despite its popularity, attempts to cultivate it in other areas were unsuccessful. Thanks to its high demand, the plant was eventually wiped out by the late second century BCE.[12]

So What Happened?

Starting with Clement of Alexandria, in the late second century CE, we start to see the idea being pressed that, if intercourse is to happen, it should be done with the intent of having children. In *The Instruction of Children* (2:10:91:2), Clement writes, "Because of its divine institution of the propagation of man, the seed is not to be vainly ejaculated, nor is it to be damaged, nor is it to be wasted."[13] In 255 CE, Hippolytus of Rome, in *Refutation of All Heresies* (9:12), writes, "On account of their prominent ancestry and great property, the so-called faithful want no children from slaves or lowborn commoners, they use drugs of sterility or bind themselves tightly in order to expel a fetus which has already been engendered [meaning 'given a soul']."[14]

With the writing of Lactantius (*Divine Institutes* 6:20) in 307 CE, we also start to see the position held by some modern-day conservatives that some people are so poor they should not procreate. In the case of Lactantius, he cautions against intercourse itself for such people, because that would risk bringing more children into the world by families that could not afford to care for them: "Wherefore, if any one on any account of poverty shall be unable to bring up children, it is better to abstain from relations with his wife." In 6:23, he states, point blank, "the genital part of the body, as the name itself teaches, has been received by us for no other purpose than the generation of offspring."[15]

The Council of Nicaea is well known by most as the meeting, organized by Constantine and attended by many early Church leaders, that helped designate the status of Jesus of Nazareth as being wholly divine and human. However, the council also discussed whether those who have been castrated could become a member of the clergy. The council states, in Canon 1, "if anyone in sound health has castrated himself, it behooves that such a one, if enrolled among the clergy, should cease ... so if any have been made eunuchs by barbarians, or by their masters, and should otherwise be found worthy, such men this canon admits to the clergy." In fact, the council decided that a castrated individual can be admitted into the clergy, so long as the individual did not voluntarily choose to castrate himself.[16]

In 419 CE, Augustine of Hippo wrote, in *Marriage and Concupiscence*, of his stern disapproval of any contraceptive methods,

> *although you are not lying [with your wife] for the sake of procreating offspring, you are not for the sake of lust obstructing their procreation with an evil prayer or an evil deed. Those who do this, although they are called husband and wife, are not; nor do they retain any reality of marriage ... they even procure poisons of sterility ... Assuredly if both husband and wife are like this, they are not married ... I dare say that the wife is in a fashion the harlot of her husband or he is an adulterer with his own wife.*[17]

During the Middle Ages, various forms of birth control were used, including coitus interruptus, the method Onan employed in the Genesis story (also known as the withdrawal method or, for some, "pull out and pray"), and placing lilly root or rue in the vagina.[18] Still, during this era the Church continued to frown upon the use of any method that prevented pregnancy and any act sex that was not intented to produce a child.[19] However, by the end of the Middle Ages, contraception had, more or less, dwindled. This is likely due to the demands on the population by all the deaths caused by the Black Plague.[20]

Still, the topic remained an important one for the Church. In 1484, for example, Pope Innocent VIII condemned contraception in *Summis desiderantes affectibus*, part of the *Malleus Maleficarum* (Witches' Hammer). In this writing, he blamed witches for "hindering men from performing the sexual act and women from conceiving."[21] In 1522, Martin Luther wrote that, what Onan did in Genesis "[was] far more atrocious than incest and adultery."[22] Even John Calvin, in his commentary on Genesis, wrote, "The voluntary spilling of semen outside of intercourse between man and woman is a monstrous thing . . . for this to extinguish the hope of the race and to kill before he is born the hoped-for offspring." Calvin felt this way specifically because he believed that marriage was "a covenant which God has consecrated." He may have been the first to express this view. The Catholic Church did not take this position until the Second Vatican Council in the twentieth century.[23]

More recently, Pope Paul VI wrote in *Humanae Vitae* (Human Life) in 1968 that it was "intrinsically wrong to use contraception," inclusive of, but not limited to, sterilization, condoms, spermicides, coitus interruptus, and the pill.[24] In

2003, Cardinal Alfonso Lopez Trujillo, who led the Vatican's Pontifical Council, told news sources that the use of condoms would spread AIDS through a false sense of security after they were recommended to people who tested positive for HIV in Africa.[25] Pope Benedict XVI stated in 2005 that condoms would "make the problem [of AIDS in Africa] worse" and offered an alternative to their recommendation, declaring that the "traditional teaching of the church has proven to be the only fail safe way to prevent the spread of HIV/AIDS."[26] While it is undeniable that abstinence is the only guaranteed way to prevent the spread of the disease sexually, it is an unrealistic ideal. As studies have shown, individuals, especially young adults, who take an abstinence pledge are more likely to have more sexual partners, be at a higher risk of contracting STIs or STDs, and have an early or unplanned pregnancy than those who don't take such a pledge.[27]

What is worse than the outright denial of the effectiveness of contraception are the counseling clincs that peddle religious ideologies and literature to turn people away from contraception rather than provide medically sound information, preventative care, and abortion. One such example is Pregnancy Services of Western Pennsylvania, a facility run by Alveda King, the niece of Martin Luther King Jr. This group caters to (mostly) impoverished women and attempts to talk the women seeking services out of abortion. It also promotes abstinence over contraception, including in lectures at public schools.[28]

Similar to the medical-sounding facilities that fail to provide proper medical advice are the "educational" reports that rail against birth control, abortion, and preventative health care. These reports, produced by fundamentalist Christians, are typically pumped through self-published "academic" journals—all of which rely on discredited science. For example, Joe McIlhaney, an evangelical Christian medical doctor with numerous books on the negative effects of sexuality in mainstream culture, published a brochure the Catholic Church would have been proud of called "Why Condoms Aren't Safe."

Such tactics are nothing in comparison to the government circus that backed abstinence-only education at the beginning of the twenty-first century. Heads of various government agencies during this time appointed by George W. Bush were members of the Christian right who favored abstinence-only education and worked hard to discredit, and even silence, sound scientific research by public health officials. They also censored data that conflicted with their ideology, especially in relation to birth control. The promotion of pseudoscience within government led the the Union of Concerned Scientists to author a March 2004 report titled *Scientific Integrity in Policy Making*. In it, the authors wrote, "There is significant evidence that the scope and scale of the manipulation, suppression, and misrepresentation of science by the Bush administration are unprecedented."[29]

Conclusion

According to the Guttmacher Institute, there are approximately 62 million women in the United States who are of "child-bearing" age (15–44 years old). Of those 62 million, 43 million are at risk of an unplanned or unintended pregnancy. In other words, almost 70 percent of women in this age group are at risk. Over the course of a year, if a sexually active woman uses no birth control, she has an 85 percent chance of becoming pregnant. Of the women at risk, those who use contraception consistently and correctly account for only 5 percent of unplanned pregnancies. So it should surprise no one that, in the 15–44 age group, roughly 99 percent of those who have had intercourse have used at least one type of birth control. Even among religious goups, 98 percent of Catholics have utilized contraceptions, as have 90 percent of Protestants.[30]

Contrary to what conservatives would like the public to think, more married couples use contraception (77 percent) than unmarried couples (42 percent). This is because married people tend to be more sexually active. Further, among those women who are on the pill, the majority (58 percent) do so for noncontraceptive purposes. This includes the use of the pill for menstrual pain, menstrual regulation, acne, and endometriosis, which in turn leads to fewer cases of anemia, ovarian cancer, and uterine cancer.[31]

The facts are clear: the use of birth control is both an appropriate means to manage reproductive health and a way for women to manage their bodies and health. Any attempt to cite the Bible to argue against the use of birth control or contraception is nothing more than grasping at straws. Very much like the biblical prohibitions against homosexuality, the biblical prohibitions against birth control are all creations of later authors and church leaders projecting their own sense of morality onto the Bible. Unfortunately this project continues today, despite the obvious benefits of birth control.

Notes

1. Cara Santa Maria, "Rush Limbaugh and Birth Control: Anti-Science on the Airwaves," *Huffington Post*, March 7, 2012, ahttp://m.huffpost.com/us/entry/1328521.

2. "Rush Limbaugh: Women Wouldn't Need Birth Control If They Simply 'Didn't Do A Certain Thing,'" Media Matters, July 2, 2014, http://mediamatters.org/video/2014/07/02/rush-women-wouldnt-need-birth-control-if-they-s/199968.

3. Bernard M. Levinson, "Deuteronomy," in *The New Oxford Annotated Bible* (New York: Oxford University Press, 2010), 291.

4. Carr, *Annotated*, 17.

5. Carr, *Annotated*, 17.

6. Carr, *Annotated*, 57.

7. Richard J. Clifford, "Psalms," in *The New Oxford Annotated Bible* (New York: Oxford University Press, 2010), 879.

8. Valerie French, "Midwives and Maternity Care in the Roman World," in *Midwifery and the Medicalization of Childbirth: Comparative Perspectives* (Hauppauge: Nova Publishers, 2004), 53.

9. Jeff Wise, "About That Overpopulation Problem," *Slate*, January 9, 2013, http://www.slate.com/articles/technology/future_tense/2013/01/world_population_may_actually_start_declining_not_exploding.html.

10. Amy Cuomo, "Birth Control," in *Encyclopedia of Motherhood* (Thousand Oaks: Sage Publications, 2010), 122–27.

11. Richard G. Lipsey, Kenneth Carlaw, and Clifford Bekar, "Historical Record on the Control of Family Size," in *Economic Transformations: General Purpose Technologies and Long-Term Economic Growth* (New York: Oxford University Press, 2005), 335–40.

12. Vern L. Bullough, "Herbal Contraceptives and Abortifacients," in *Encyclopedia of Birth Control* (Santa Barbara: ABC-CLIO, 2001), 125–28.

13. Jason T. Adams, *Called to Give Life: A Sourcebook on the Blessings of Children and the Harm of Contraception* (Dayton: One More Soul Publishers, 2003), 23.

14. Stephen E. Lammers and Allen Verhey, *On Moral Medicine: Theological Perspectives in Medical Ethics* (Grand Rapids: Wm. B. Eerdmans Publishing, 1998), 594.

15. John Salza, "Contraception," Scripture Catholic, http://www.scripturecatholic.com/contraception.html (accessed October 27, 2014).

16. Salza, "Contraception."

17. As quoted in Robert Jutte, *Contraception: A History* (Cambridge: Polity Press, 2008), 26.

18. Lianne McTavish, "Contraception and Birth Control," in *Encyclopedia of Women in the Renaissance: Italy, France, and England* (Santa Barbara: ABC-CLIO, 2007), 91–92.

19. Cuomo, *Motherhood*, 121–26.

20. John M. Riddle, *Eve's Herbs: A History of Contraception and Abortion in the West* (Cambridge: Harvard University Press, 1999), 169–207.

21. Alan Charles Kors and Edward Peters, *Witchcraft in Europe, 400–1700: A Documentary History* (Philadelphia: University of Pennsylvania Press, 2001), 177–80.

22. Theresa Notare, *"A Revolution in Christian Morals," Lambeth 1930–Resolution #15. History and Reception* (Ann Arbor: Proquest, 2008), 147.

23. Adrian Thatcher, *God, Sex, and Gender: An Introduction* (Hoboken: Wiley Publishers, 2011), 101–2.

24. Robert H Brom, Bishop of San Diego, "Birth Control," Catholic Answers to Explain and Defend the Faith, August 10, 2004, http://www.catholic.com//tracts/birth-control (accessed October 27, 2014).

25. "Pope: Condoms Could Worsen Aids," *Al Jazeera*, March 18, 2009, http://www.aljazeera.com/news/africa/2009/03/2009 3183550676229.html (accessed October 27, 2014).

26. Riazat Butt, "Pope Claims Condoms Could Make African Aids Crisis Worse," *Guardian*, March 17, 2009, http://www. theguardian.com/world/2009/mar/17/pope-africa-condoms-aids.

27. Beth Leyba, "Abstinence-Only Education Doesn't Work—I Know from Personal Experience," *Huffington Post*, March 4, 2014, http://www.huffingtonpost.com/beth-leyba/abstinence-only-education_b_4896696.html.

28. Hedges, *Fascists*, 41.

29. As quoted in Hedges, *Fascists*, 122, 126.

30. "Fact Sheet: Contraceptive Use in the United States," Guttmacher Institute, http://guttmacher.org/pubs/fb_contr_use. html (accessed December 27, 2014).

31. "Fact Sheet," Guttmacher Institute; "Non-Contraceptive Benefits of the Birth Control Pill," American Society for Reproductive Medicine, http://asrm.org/FACTSHEET_ noncontraceptive_Benefits_of_Birth_control_pills/ (accessed October 23, 2014).

Epilogue

The Bible has some rather interesting points on sex and sexuality. They are not the points that modern-day moralists, or the Church, make, but they are interesting nonetheless. It is rife with references to sex. Much of its lessons related to sex derive from the era in which it was written and have to do with issues of paternity, the family line, and economic stability. Nowhere in the Bible do we find recommendations or prescriptions for men to punish women, to impose a dress code on them, or to make decisions for them without letting them decide for themselve—or, at the very least, without including them in the conversation.

Neither does the Bible communicate a prohibition against homosexuality. Rather, it prohibits certain acts connected with foreign cultures and the worshipping of "false idols"— which together posed a threat to the Israelites and their own god, Yahweh. Regardless, any prohibitions that do exist in the Bible are products of a particular time and place. Given how our species has evolved and learned and created new tools and practices that help us live longer and with greater comfort, the Bible's prohibitions, laws, and commands about sex and sexual practices that do exist are no longer relevant. For an ancient people, a bride's virginity mattered for purposes of ensuring a groom's paternity of a child. Today, with effective birth control methods and technology that allows tests for paternity, ancient views about the importance of premarital virginity can and should be thrown aside and ignored.

So-called biblical arguments used to prohibit the use of contraception and other practices are misplaced and not grounded in the Bible's actual lessons and meaning. The story of Onan, for example, has to do with the tradition of levirate marriage and is not meant as a prohibition on birth control or contraception—in fact, no contraception is used in the story. The Bible also lacks any reference to abortion, even though it was a common practice before, during, and after the Bible was written. Among those who oppose abortion on religious grounds today, how many know that? People take the stories as handed down to them from people just as misinformed as they are and cite them without questioning or considering their original intent or context. Such misunderstanding does not end with what has been discussed in this book. For example, negative views toward masturbation also mistakenly stem from the Onan story. Any attempt to address other such topics would require nothing more than a reiteration of the subject matter and biblical passages already covered.

What it all comes down to is that modern moralists, be they priests, politicians, evangelists, or "sidewalk counselors," have no idea what they are talking about. But, in many respects, the damage has already been done. Many of their messages, often left unchallenged, have filtered throughout our culture. So, what is it that we can do to make a change? Understanding the problem is the first step. No change can occur unless it begins with you. By becoming aware of the problem, we can model the change we wish to see in others and in the world. Be conscious of how you feel and think when you observe how people appear, dress, or act. Think before you speak: will your comments be interpreted as sexist? Privileged? Homophobic? Transphobic? Are you ignorant of the positions and lives of those you are speaking with—or about? Even with the writing of this book, I made sure to get the opinions of those I was writing about to ensure I was not speaking from a privileged, uninformed position. It would have been ridiculous for me to do otherwise. Similarly, I ask that, in your journey to make a change, you educate yourself—do your own research, read other books, and have conversations with those whose position you have not experienced. It will not be an overnight change, or even an easy one, but it is the best place to start.

After that, try to remain informed about what is going on in the world—and vote. The 2014 U.S. midterm elections saw some of the lowest turnout ever. The effects are far-reaching. Due to the small turnout, individuals who wish to enact policies that would harm the reproductive rights of women came to power. For example, in Colorado, Democratic senator Mark Udall was defeated by Republican candidate Corey Gardner, who ran an anti-abortion campaign and wants to change the definition of "personhood" to make abortion equated with murder.[1] The results likely would have been quite different had the voter turnout been like what we see for sporting events or the release of new electronic devices.

We have, for too long now, permitted antiquated views, as promoted and championed by the religious right, to take hold over our culture and society. We have permitted the Church to dictate how we should behave with regard to sex and our bodies and have followed prohibitions declared by people who have taken a life-long vow of celibacy. These are the same people who have told us, time and again, that chastity is the only form of birth control that should be permitted, but who still believe a virgin gave birth two thousand years ago. Think about that for a moment. Would we accept driving instructions from someone who had never set foot in a car? Would we follow only those recipes written by people who had never tasted food? We have been doing it wrong. And for far too long.

We must become better informed than those trying to tell us what is right or wrong with regard to sexuality, sexual identity, or sexual activity. We need to approach all claims with skepticism, to do our own research, and to become better able to identify statements of fact from opinion. We live in an age of information, but information does not equate to knowledge. We can be "informed" by listening to the Pat Robertsons and Jerry Falwells of the world, or we can gain knowledge by opening books, reading studies, and listening to educated opinions surrounding the topics the modern moralists love to preach about. But, the journey does not include waiting for others to give us what we need to be prepared. We need to seek out the information ourselves and put it in to action. If we become informed and motivate one another to become active when situations arise that require action, then we truly will see a change.

Notes

1.   Michaela Cohen, "What the Mid-Term Elections Mean for Reproductive Rights: A Growing Threat," National Organization for Women, November 17, 2014, http://now.org/blog/what-the-mid-term-elections-mean-for-reproductive-rights-a-growing-threat/.

Acknowledgments

To my wife and children, thank you for your continued and unending encouragement for all that I do. I appreciate your patience and understanding with the work I do. I love you all and am so lucky to have you.

To my colleagues, Dan Arel, Joshua Kelly, and J. D. Brucker, you gentlemen always keep me on my toes and make me strive for excellence in what I do. I admire you for the work you do, for the gold you churn out, and for considering me a friend. Thanks for your continued support, in as many forms as it comes.

To Pitchstone, for publishing excellent works and for considering my work worthy to sit in your catalog. I am humbled and excited to have such a great working relationship with a wonderful publishing group. Thank you for all you do.

About the Author

Matthew O'Neil is an activist, theologian, and teacher. He has his MA in theology from Saint Michael's College with graduate certification in Mediation and Applied Conflict Studies, and he is a certified Humanist chaplain and celebrant through the American Humanist Association. He is the author of *You Say That I Am: Jesus and the Messianic Problem* and writes for the *Danthropology* blog through the Patheos network. He lives in Saint Albans, Vermont, with his wife and children.